HUTZLER'S

The Hutzler family of stores, circa 1980. *Clockwise from top*: Downtown, Westview, Eastpoint, Towson, Inner Harbor, Service Building, Southdale and Salisbury. *Courtesy of Jacques Kelly*.

HUTZLER'S

WHERE BALTIMORE SHOPS

MICHAEL J. LISICKY

Charleston · London

THE
History
PRESS

Published by The History Press
Charleston, SC 29403
www.historypress.net

Copyright © 2009 by Michael J. Lisicky
All rights reserved

First published 2009, Second printing 2009, Third printing 2009,
Fourth printing 2010, Fifth printing 2010, Sixth printing 2010,
Seventh printing 2011

Manufactured in the United States

ISBN 978.1.59629.828.6

Library of Congress Cataloging-in-Publication Data
Lisicky, Michael J.
Hutzler's : where Baltimore shops / Michael J. Lisicky.
p. cm.
Includes bibliographical references.
ISBN 978-1-59629-828-6
1. Hutzler's (Firm)--History. 2. Department stores--Maryland--Baltimore--History. 3.
Baltimore (Md.)--History. I. Title.
HF5465.U6H96 2009
381'.141097526--dc22
2009039528

To my mother, who taught me about loyalty and identity.

CONTENTS

FOREWORD

Years after the store closed, I confess to remaining in a state of withdrawal about the passing of Hutzler's. On a Saturday at about 10:30 a.m., I find myself asking why I'm not downtown, Howard and Saratoga Streets, having a fabulous time. I'd usually arrive on a Baltimore Transit Co. bus. From Liberty Street, I'd look westward through tiny Clay Street and glance at the big bronze vertical lettering saying the family name. North Building. South Building. Annex. These were my addresses.

I consider myself lucky to have known the store for forty years. My earliest recollection was of the downstairs luncheonette and hearing the Baltimore and Ohio Railroad trains rumble underneath. There I'd be having the vegetable soup (world's best) and fruit cup with raspberry ice cream and maybe a taste of my grandmother's chocolate ice cream soda made by a talented worker we knew only as Celeste. She dipped and fizzed behind the fountain. The day the Howard Street store closed was so abysmal, I don't like to think about it.

Baltimoreans were quite proud to have a Hutzler Brothers Co. as part of their city world. It was a store that was better than it needed to be. It did not sell frivolous, unnecessary merchandise. The place was spacious, clean and appealingly fresh. It was obvious that care was taken to display and arrange merchandise. It was sensible without being dowdy. The place treated its customers with courtesy and respect. I'm told there was a staff member who combed the obituary columns to spot the deaths of customers. The survivor received a handwritten sympathy note. The whole encounter elevated shopping to a better level. We had favorite salespeople who possessed a breezy esprit de corps. We often had private nicknames for them as well, especially if they resembled certain character actors and actresses. It was comforting in the world of the 1960s to enter the store and know that the same familiar face would be behind that certain counter.

What do I miss about Hutzler's? For starters, the coffee chiffon pie from the Quixie restaurant. When that particular lunch area closed about 1972, I wrote a two-page letter of complaint. I also received a speedy reply.

Where is the 1940s-styled lettering spelling out "Down Escalator"? The elevators had bronze eagles on the doors on the sixth floor. Around the edges of the tearoom were cranberry-colored hurricane lamp globes. People were having their sandwiches on cheese toast. The waitresses wore gray uniforms and white aprons. There was a kind of public parlor, with upholstered chairs and framed prints of old Baltimore. There were telephone booths and tables to write letters. The woman in charge would provide a piece of paper and envelope. No charge.

Hutzler's glorious toy department had been an old Eutaw Street theatre, converted into retail uses in the 1930s. It had all the modernist styling touches that forward-looking architects had in their bag of tricks. There was a swirling ramp up to the phonograph record department. Coves held indirect lighting to illuminate the displays that some artist had created around the edges of this amazing chamber.

As you entered the salesroom, windows offered a preview of what the aisles and shelves held. Everything was painted pink, with a contrasting tone of coral for the handrails and cabinets.

In those days, merchants didn't believe they had to stockpile everything so high that it resembled a warehouse. Today, we gladly shop with metal carts in warehouses in search of low prices. Bar codes and inventory control are what Art Deco decor and imported German toys used to be. Every so often there was a table full of stuff that some buyer could have only picked up on an expedition to the Old World. I recall what seemed like one thousand little handmade houses, each with a price tag, and how I wanted to possess one of each. I looked and looked again. Each was different. I settled on one, cheap but representative. It still rests in my cellar. Don't ask me to find it.

Jacques Kelly

ACKNOWLEDGEMENTS

I would like to thank the following people who helped to make this book become my personal "Occasion Extraordinaire": Jacques Kelly, who opened his home and collection and truly made this book complete and personal; Dan and Sue Sachs for helping me get the ball rolling and contributing so much to this publication; John Waters for his witty insights; George Bernstein; Richard Hutzler; Jiggs Hutzler; Bunny Hutzler; Rosemary Hutzler; David Hutzler; Gilbert Sandler; Senator Barbara Mikulski; the Office of the Mayor of Baltimore; Sheila Dixon; Lainy Lebow Sachs; and Governor William Donald Schaefer.

Thanks and appreciation go to the staff of the Maryland Historical Society, the staff of the Maryland Department at the Enoch Pratt Free Library, Richard Parsons and Jason Domasky of the Baltimore County Public Library, Rachel Kassman and the staff of the Jewish Museum of Maryland, Allen Feiler of the *Baltimore Jewish Times* and Catherine Scott of the Baltimore Museum of Industry. A big thank-you must go to Jan Whitaker, who got me involved in this project to begin with. A deep appreciation goes to Susan Rome, Steve Mogge and Kevin Mueller for their assistance and contributions. And a special thanks to the countless Hutzlerites and Baltimoreans who shared their personal memories and stories of this great Baltimore department store with me.

And a deep sincere appreciation and affection to my wife Sandy, who never made me feel odd or uncomfortable with this somewhat unusual interest in department stores, and who helped make this book readable. And to my daughter Jordan, who always allowed her father to stop the car and take a picture of any department store he finds "along the way."

INTRODUCTION

I don't quite understand my passion for department stores. I think I'll blame it on my mother. When I was a child, my mother would pack the car with my brothers and me and we would be off on a road trip that usually centered on shopping. I didn't necessarily enjoy the shopping, but I did love spending time with my family while discovering new cities, new restaurants and new stores.

I grew up in southern New Jersey, directly across the river from Philadelphia. My mother loved Philadelphia's Strawbridge & Clothier department store. Her first job was at Strawbridge's and for a number of years she sang in the Strawbridge & Clothier Chorus. She eventually stopped working at the store but it was always "her store." Even as a small child, I always knew when it was Clover Day at Strawbridge's. Clover Day was a tradition, and that's what Strawbridge & Clothier stood for—tradition.

There were other stores in Philadelphia. My mother bought her shoes and tires for the car at Lit Brothers. She also spent a lot of time buying her kids' clothes in Gimbels' Budget Store. (I don't think I even went to the main floor of Gimbels until I graduated from high school.) We also had John Wanamaker, but for some reason it always seemed out of our reach. I don't know quite why.

When you live in the Philadelphia area, you can travel to many different cities, large and small, within a two-hour drive. I loved how each city seemed to have its own personality. Since my mother would always take us shopping, I always paid attention to the different stores. I loved all of the different names.

I loved all of the different logos. I truly felt like I was "out of town." When I saw Hess's, I knew we were in Allentown. When I saw Dunham's, I knew we were in Trenton. When I saw Hutzler's, I knew we were in Baltimore.

Hutzler's always seemed so invincible. Its Downtown store seemed so monumental yet personal. As a child, I was always concerned how Clay Street ran right through the building. I was also a little scared at the way the store spelled out HUTZLER with its Art Deco lettering. (I always thought, "Why not Hutzler's?") No visit to Baltimore was complete without a stop at the Towson Hutzler's on the way back home. At the time, it seemed that Towson was nothing more than Towson University and Hutzler's. I couldn't imagine that that would ever change.

Things did change. Society changed, and so did the way the country did its business. By the 1980s, department stores were on notice. Their slice of the market was severely shrinking. Shopping became less personal. Department store buildings were getting older and becoming expensive to operate. As some stores became stronger, others became weaker. Unfortunately, Hutzler's, the store that defined Baltimore to me, became weak and was barely able to make it out of the 1980s.

I always saw Hutzler's as the Strawbridge & Clothier of Baltimore. Good merchandise, good service, loyal customers. Unfortunately, both Hutzler's and Strawbridge's are gone, as well as most department stores of my youth. I miss these stores. I miss their names, their logos and their candy counters. Nothing is forever, and I guess that was true about Hutzler's. But I'll always miss those special day trips. It was a different time.

This book will hopefully bring back some of those special memories of Hutzler's that made the store a Baltimore institution. Twenty years after its doors closed, the store is still grieved by many people. I miss Hutzler's and I also miss those special car rides with my mother.

A WORD FROM JOHN WATERS

To me, Hutzler's was always the A-list store, and I think everybody knew that. Hutzler's was always a step above the other three stores. It was a class act. No matter what family you were in, from whatever economic background, Hutzler's was always thought of as the best store.

Hutzler's Downtown was the one I liked best and I loved the Tea Room. I used to go to the store downtown but I remember Hutzler's Towson because I grew up in Lutherville. I remember when it opened. I used to hang out after school with other semi-juvenile delinquents in the doorway that led right outside where the Towson Movies is. The store detective there knew us and hated us because we did shoplift. (I remember shoplifting an outfit right off the mannequin.) We hung out in that doorway every day after school. That was our clubhouse and they couldn't do anything about it because we weren't in or out of the store. Later, Hutzler's was the only store where I actually spent money. The only time that I ever bought something "designer" was at Hutzler's. I think they broke even on me.

I think people were really sad when Hutzler's closed because they had a great many personal memories being there with their families. Hutzler's lasted longer than most things when you think about it. They had a great run, and that's why people are so nostalgic about it. I don't think you're going to get anybody to say, "I hated shopping at Hutzler's." It was the best we had. There wasn't anything better.

June 30, 2009

SETTING UP SHOP

"U ncle Abe was kindly, decently affectionate and supposedly principled, just like the whole damn family was," Richard Hutzler recalls affectionately.[1] Richard was eight years old when Hutzler's founder, Abram G. Hutzler, passed away in 1927. It was Abram, along with his two brothers, who built a retail dynasty on Baltimore's Howard Street. For generations, the name "Hutzler" was synonymous with Baltimore retailing.

Abram Hutzler's father, Moses, was born in 1800 in Hagenbach, a village in Bavaria, Germany. He was a merchant by trade, and in 1838 Moses set sail "on a frail sailing vessel" with his young son, Abram, and settled near Frederick, Maryland, in order to start a new life.[2] Within a few years, Moses moved to Baltimore, where he set up shop on Eutaw Street. But it didn't take long before the retailing bug bit Abram, along with his brothers Charles and David.

In July 1858, Moses Hutzler signed the paperwork for his son Abram to open his own small store on the corner of Howard and Clay Streets. Abram was too young to do business in his own name, so the store operated as M. Hutzler & Son. The store did a respectable business but hit its first bump in April 1861, when fighting erupted on Pratt Street and brought forth the first casualties of America's Civil War. Commerce in Baltimore was paralyzed, but Hutzler's continued to operate. Within a year, the business recovered and the store found its way back on the road to prosperity.

His brothers joined Abram in the business. While David minded the storefront on Howard Street, Abram and Charles branched out and ran a

Stonework of the top of Hutzler's 1888 Palace building. *Courtesy of Jacques Kelly.*

wholesale business on Baltimore Street. However, it was the retail business that flourished, and Abram and Charles returned to Howard Street to concentrate on the retail operation. The Hutzler brothers operated their store as a "One-Price House" in order to address the injustice that became apparent through persistent bargaining from its various customers.

In the 1870s, Hutzler's began giving its five female clerks a dime every morning for the purchase "of an apple or two." This practice was the forbear of Hutzler's establishment of a medical department in later years.[3]

Hutzler's began to expand in 1874 with the purchase of a neighboring building. In 1881, the store again expanded, and by 1887 three additional properties along Howard Street had been purchased. The brothers knew that it was time to build a new structure that would suit its expanding business.[4]

BUILDING A PALACE

In 1888, Hutzler's opened its new structure, which was so ornate that it was dubbed a "palace." The five-story building, designed by the architectural firm Baldwin and Pennington, was built of Nova Scotia gray stone and was carved with arabesque heads and foliage. Large display windows brought in plenty of sunlight. But perhaps one of the greatest features of the building was the carved keystone likeness of Moses Hutzler, which was set above a display window on Clay Street. The store employed two hundred workers and housed two passenger elevators. The practice of exchanging unsatisfactory merchandise or refunding cash was established.[5] The business consisted of many departments, and it was especially proud of its cloak and dress department. Its lace department boasted the largest selection south of New York.

On March 2, 1908, Hutzler's officially celebrated its fiftieth anniversary. Abram and David were there to shake each customer's hand. To honor this momentous occasion, artist Harrison Fisher was commissioned to paint his vision of a typical Baltimore girl. This portrait, used in promotion at the time, was a source of pride throughout the store's history. Hutzler's spectacular Palace building, the savvy management that helped it survive the Civil War, its home delivery system and its groundbreaking advertising methods were all celebrated. The year 1908 also marked the incorporation of the Hutzler Brothers Company.[6]

The population of Maryland continued to grow, and so did Hutzler's as it tried to meet the needs of an expanding customer base. Even with

Above: Early structures of Hutzler Brothers await demolition for the building of the 1888 Palace store. The building on the far right was the original Hutzler Brothers store of 1858. *Courtesy of Jacques Kelly.*

Left: The 1888 Palace building as seen in the early 1900s. *Courtesy of the Baltimore County Public Library Legacy Web.*

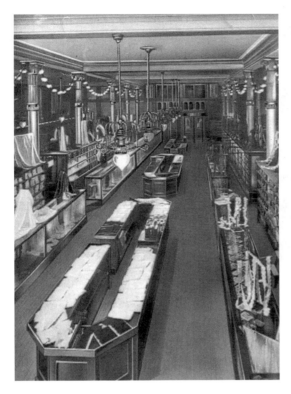

Left: Bird's-eye view of the main aisle of Hutzler's Palace store, circa early 1900s. *Courtesy of the Baltimore County Public Library Legacy Web*.

Below: The main aisle of Hutzler's Palace featuring bric-a-brac, circa early 1900s. *Courtesy of the Baltimore County Public Library Legacy Web*.

The silk fabrics department at Hutzler's Palace, circa early 1900s. *Courtesy of the Baltimore County Public Library Legacy Web.*

World War I raging across the ocean, the company built its first major building after the Palace in 1916. A five-story structure was erected on Saratoga Street and two additional properties on Howard Street became occupied that same year. At the time, business was booming and profits were large. "They must have made money hand over fist in those days," says Richard Hutzler.

In 1919, Albert Hutzler Sr. became president and the company began to truly prosper. Hutzler's introduced its first company magazine, *Tips and Taps*, in March 1921. Over 1,500 names were suggested for the publication's name, but it was William Maben in the advertising office who won the honor of coining the magazine. The name described the act of giving an employer a "tip" to achieve better store performance and then having the employer give a shoulder "tap" for a job well done.[7]

At age eighty-two, Abram was honored for building "a superstructure of an enterprise which has become something more than a mere mercantile experiment. He and his associates have made it veritably an institution characteristic of the fine traditions of the commercial life of the city in which it grew and flourished."

In 1924, the Saratoga Street building was expanded from five to ten stories. The original Palace, or South Building, was also enlarged. Hutzler's planned to create a large, uniform, L-shaped structure connecting Saratoga Street to

Women's suits featured at Hutzler's Palace, circa early 1900s. *Courtesy of the Baltimore County Public Library Legacy Web.*

Howard Street, but this grand plan for renovation never came to fruition. The store always occupied many different buildings that never achieved any type of uniform appearance.

In the fall of 1927, store founder Abram's health took a sharp downward turn. On October 6, 1927, he established the endowment of the Abram G. Hutzler Chair of Political Economy at Johns Hopkins University. Over the years, the Hutzler family was very loyal to Johns Hopkins. Unfortunately, four days after establishing the endowment, Abram became gravely ill, and the man who established the business in 1858 from a one-room storefront on Howard Street passed from the retail scene.

The year 1929 saw the country enter the Great Depression. Amazingly, Hutzler's continued to expand and progress, including the debut of the Saratoga Street garage and the underground tunnel to the main store. Richard Hutzler recalls, "I have to confess that we suffered little hardship in the family [during those times]." The timing could not have been better for Hutzler's next venture. On September 28, 1929, Hutzler's opened its Downstairs Store. The Downstairs Store was basically an economy store that had its own lines of merchandise—a "Thrift Store with Hutzler Standards."[8] "They made it very clear that it was not a bargain basement," says Richard Hutzler. At one time, the Downstairs Store even had its own separate entrance. The store, known for its plainer

The planned 1924 expansion of Hutzler's that would have given the store a uniform appearance. This expansion never occurred. The original Palace building is seen on the left. *Courtesy of Jacques Kelly.*

and dowdier goods, developed a loyal following. In some ways, Hutzler's was now catering to two different types of customers with its Upstairs and Downstairs Stores.

Upstairs, innovative merchandise was featured. In 1930, the first commercially available sports car was displayed. The car was small enough to drive down the main aisle in the store. It was able to reach speeds up to ninety-one miles per hour and could hold one gallon of gas, which could take it fifty-one miles. It cost the Hutzler customer $6,000. Though none were purchased, the "buzz" generated was noteworthy. In 1931, the Home Department introduced the new "electric refrigerator," destined "no doubt to become a necessity in every modern home."[9]

THE GLORY DAYS

With its excellent service and the prestige of its name, Hutzler's was the closest Baltimoreans got to haute couture.
—*Gilbert Sandler, Baltimore historian*

October 11, 1931, saw Hutzler's greatest feat to date. In the midst of the Depression, Hutzler's embarked on the largest building operation in the city. The five-story building was an Art Deco masterpiece. With its new slogan, "A Maryland Institution," Hutzler's welcomed fifty thousand people to its grand opening. Mayor Howard W. Jackson stressed, "Hutzler Brothers establishment is a made-in-Baltimore product." Governor Albert C. Ritchie declared that it was "a Baltimore institution rather than a Baltimore business house." "Greater Hutzler's," as it was known, now spread throughout six structures. The 1924 plan of building one uniform structure had been abandoned. But that didn't matter, as people still flocked to Hutzler's.[10]

In addition to all of the opening festivities, Hutzler's also opened Baltimore's first escalator, which remained in the memories of many after the store finally closed. Buyer Sue Gaston Sachs remembers the narrow old wooden escalator with its "big teeth." "It scared me as a little kid!" The escalators, with their creaking wood treads, transported customers from the main floor up to the fourth floor. Escalators made from steel served the fifth and sixth floors.

The famous Art Deco structure of Hutzler's that opened in 1932. The Palace is seen on the left. The new structure was built right on top of Clay Street. *Courtesy of Jacques Kelly.*

Baltimore celebrated the new Hutzler building. The *Baltimore Sun* ran an editorial under the caption "Living Up to Tradition." The editorial went on to say:

> *In these days when so many are finding it hard to keep their chins up, and when men forget that the American people have shown in all their periods of stress and the victories that stamina has won, it is refreshing and encouraging to turn one's eyes to what Hutzler Brothers' Company has done. In the midst of the depression that Baltimore firm has flung a challenge into the faces of the Jeremiahs, has affirmed its faith in the future and has demonstrated the reality of its professions by adding 50,000 square feet of space to the area in which it offers merchandise to the people of Baltimore. It is the kind of steady faith, the kind of surefooted action, that we like to believe is characteristic of this well-bottomed old town.*

Hutzler's began its tradition of distributing calendars of local artists in 1938 and continued until 1975. The calendars shown are from 1938 of the Washington Monument, 1942 of the latest construction to the downtown Hutzler's store, 1949 of the Baltimore Symphony at the Lyric Opera House and 1975 of the main entrance to Johns Hopkins University. *Private collection.*

Festivities continued as Hutzler's celebrated its Diamond Jubilee in 1933. Boasting "75 Years of Leadership," Hutzler's held an Anniversary Exposition with exhibits and demonstrations including modern inventions such as the fluorescent light bulb and the dial telephone. Also, a 75 Year Club was established for customers who were seventy-five years and older.

Hutzler's provided many special services for its employees and customers. As early as 1929, an employee credit union was established. The store came out of the Depression in good shape. Former vice-president and treasurer George Hutzler Bernstein says that Hutzler's "must have been making great profits back in the '20s and the '30s." In 1938, the company decided to advance tuition to its employees who were taking night courses at educational institutions such as Johns Hopkins University, the Maryland Institute and the University of Maryland. Approximately two dollars were deducted from each week's paycheck for each course successfully completed. The employee was then refunded part of the amount of tuition, up to ten dollars per year. A primitive healthcare plan was established—a doctor offered free medical advice to employees between the hours of 9:30 a.m. and noon. The company also offered a "competent dentist" on certain mornings at reasonable prices. Employee discounts were granted for purchases made by the worker and his

A view of Hutzler's fur salon featuring ashtrays, circa 1940. *Courtesy of Jacques Kelly.*

or her dependants. Any attempt to purchase merchandise for friends or relatives was considered "equivalent to dishonesty."[11] Beginning in 1938, Hutzler's offered customers a free yearly calendar that featured scenes of Baltimore and Maryland crafted by local artists. This tradition continued for decades.

By 1940, Hutzler's was one of Baltimore's major employers. The store employed approximately 1,500 workers and continued to grow. Hutzler's announced in July 1941 that it would add five more stories to its 1932 building on Howard Street. The additional 40,000 square feet of selling space brought the total sales space of the

Hutzler's continues to expand in July 1941 as five stories are added to the main building. *Courtesy of the BGE collection at the Baltimore Museum of Industry.*

store to about 220,000 square feet. Hutzler's proclaimed that this expansion was a "synonym of progress and prestige."

And then came World War II. Soon, the store began to lose some of its men to the Armed Forces. The July 1942 issue of *Tips and Taps* announced, "This is our war—Nothing must stand in the way of our ultimate victory."

The finished product, the 1942 completion of the Hutzler Bros. complex on Howard Street. *Courtesy of Jacques Kelly.*

The publication further declared that "rationing is good" and that the war brought "new friends through car pools and healthier diets through the shortage of sugar."[12]

Hutzler's Victory Window was the first of its kind in the country. Starting on January 9, 1942, the store helped sell war bonds directly from one of its display windows on Howard Street. In the first year alone, over $2 million of bonds were sold, eliciting a citation from the secretary of the treasury. By the time the Victory Window closed, over $18 million of war bonds had been sold. During the war, 276 Hutzlerites served in the various theaters of battle. Only 3 workers lost their lives.[13]

Scarcities were felt everywhere from the war. Possibly the most bizarre story came from a woman who had parked her car in the Saratoga Street garage. She had been hoarding gasoline and had stored twenty gallons of gasoline in containers left on the back seat of her car. The heat of the day caused the gasoline to ignite, causing minor damage to her car. Even with her possible catastrophic action averted, the woman threatened to sue the store.[14]

FOREWORD

The formation of an organization against enemy air raids has been completed. Naturally it was a new experience for us at Hutzler's and we little thought that it was one we would ever have to do. It was no easy task, and weeks of planning and work were necessary.

Our duty is to protect the lives and limbs of our employees and customers in addition to our property, if and when enemy air raids occur in Baltimore.

Our plans will succeed or fail in direct ratio to the performance of each individual in our Air Raid Protection (A. R. P.) pyramids.

The men and women chosen to be the leaders in our A. R. P. organization have been carefully selected, and we can rely upon them to carry on with calm courage when emergency arises. Our greatest danger will be from panic and not, we sincerely believe, from a bomb, fire or explosion. Therefore we urge you to—

Learn Your Duties
Practice Your Assignments
and Above All
KEEP COOL!

February, 1942

HUTZLER BROTHERS ℂ

Left: Hutzler's prepares its employees for a possible attack during World War II with this booklet dating from February 1942. *Private collection.*

Below: Hutzler's fights the war by promoting the sale of war bonds. *Courtesy of the Maryland Historical Society.*

When Baltimore Thinks of Quality
It Thinks of Hutzler's

The store celebrated its ninetieth anniversary in 1948 with the theme "When Baltimore Thinks of Quality, It Thinks of Hutzler's." *Courtesy of the Jewish Museum of Maryland, 207.029.033.*

The next milestone in Hutzler's history was its ninetieth anniversary, commemorated in 1948. Under the byline "A Maryland Institution Salutes Maryland's Past and Present," the store celebrated Baltimore's leading companies and institutions through displays in its windows and newspaper advertisements. But Hutzler's would also not let people forget that "When Baltimore Thinks of Quality, It Thinks of Hutzler's."

Hutzler's ended the 1940s poised for still more growth but looking past downtown. One of its neighboring competitors had already started opening stores in Baltimore's near suburbs, and Hutzler's had to react before it was too late.

SHOPPING AROUND

Across the country, families of Jewish merchants helped establish what became the modern department store. Jewish merchants were common in Eastern Europe, and Jewish businesses helped establish culture and employment for their community. Many Jewish families were philanthropic and were seen as leaders in their communities. This was true in Baltimore.[15]

Baltimore was by no means a one-store town. A number of large-scale merchants located their businesses near the intersection of Howard and Lexington Streets. This was where people were, where people started and ended their shopping for the day.

By the late 1940s, Howard and Lexington Streets was considered "the crossroads of Maryland." It was said that "here meet the wives of Baltimore brokers, of Eastern Shore chicken farmers, of Western Maryland miners, of Southern Maryland manufacturers. Here meet the teacher and the student, housewife and business woman."[16] Interestingly enough, Hutzler's was not located directly on the corner of Howard and Lexington. It was located one short block north at Howard and Clay Streets, but its signature Art Deco building with its brass HUTZLER letters towered above the intersection. One didn't have to travel far to find its nearest competitor, Hochschild Kohn.

HOCHSCHILD, KOHN & CO.

Max Hochschild initially opened his "one-price store" on Gay Street in 1876. Twenty years later, as focus on Howard Street intensified, Hochschild's left

The busy intersection of Howard and Lexington Streets, circa 1956. The image shows Gutman's and Kresge's on the right and Stewart's on the far left. *Courtesy of Jacques Kelly.*

its Gay Street location. Joining with the Kohn brothers, Benno and Louis, Hochschild, Kohn & Co., Baltimore's newest "palace" department store, opened its doors on November 15, 1897. Located at the corner of Howard and Lexington Streets, the building was designed by architect Joseph Sperry. The structure expanded in 1912 and a sixth story was added. By 1947, Hochschild Kohn encompassed five buildings and served as a main anchor to the famous intersection.[17]

Beyond the retail competition that existed between Hochschild's and Hutzler's, the two department store giants had other, more personal, ties. Max Hochschild's daughter, Gretchen, was married to Albert Hutzler Sr. Max Hochschild's wife was Lina Hamburger from the retail store Isaac Hamburger & Son. Isaac Hamburger had founded one of America's oldest clothiers in Baltimore back in 1850. "The whole Jewish department store business in Baltimore was very incestuous," says George Hutzler Bernstein.

Though Hochschild's had the corner location and the parade, it was always seen as a step or two below Hutzler's in quality. *Sun* reporter Jacques

Kelly states, "Hochschild Kohn was a frumpier store, but there are a lot of frumpy people in Baltimore. Hochschild's frumpiness was kind of fun." When it came to his own shopping needs, Governor William Donald Schaefer preferred Hochschild's to Hutzler's. "Hutzler's was the premier store. Hochschild's was for common people like me. I'm a common person. I curse and I drink. Oh my, I'm a horrible man," says Schaefer.

Though it could be argued that it was not the store that Hutzler's was, Hochschild's was actually more innovative than its competition. In June 1947, Hochschild Kohn opened one of the nation's earliest branch department stores at the Edmondson Village Shopping Center in West Baltimore. That was soon followed by another branch in November 1948 at York Road and Belvedere Avenue. During the 1950s, Hochschild's located stores at Eastpoint (1956) and in one of the nation's first enclosed shopping malls, Harundale Mall (1958.) In 1966, the descendants of the Hochschild and Kohn families sold the firm to Diversified Retailing. Three years later, Supermarkets General took control of the company. It attempted, unsuccessfully, to expand into York, Pennsylvania, and Columbia, Maryland, before it was forced to reevaluate its market and its Downtown store.[18]

Street scene of Hochschild Kohn and Hutzler's from June 14, 1973. *Courtesy of the BGE collection at the Baltimore Museum of Industry.*

STEWART & CO.

Stewart & Co. was located on the northeast corner of Howard and Lexington Streets. Its signature white "palace" was built in 1900, originally the home of another retail establishment, Posner Brothers. Samuel Posner was a longtime Baltimore merchant, but the move and construction costs of this new building at Howard and Lexington proved dire. After rumors circulated about Posner's financial troubles, it was announced on December 20, 1901, that Posner's would be sold to Associated Merchants Company. AMC's negotiator for the deal was Louis Stewart, the owner of New York's James McCreery & Co. store. In March 1902, the business officially became Stewart & Co.[19]

Stewart's managed a quality store but always seemed to be in Hutzler's shadow. It never received the loyal following that the other stores enjoyed. Perhaps that was due to the fact that an established Jewish Baltimore family was not operating Stewart's.

Stewart's found its way to the suburbs and spared no expense in the stores' construction. In 1953, it announced plans for a large branch on York Road near the Towson border. Famed architect Raymond Loewy designed this store, as well as some of the other branches. The York Road branch remained Stewart's largest volume store for decades. In 1960, Associated Dry Goods, parent of Lord & Taylor, purchased the business. Stewart's continued its trek to the suburbs, with locations on Reisterstown Road, at the Westview and Golden Ring Malls and in Timonium.

Stewart's York Road store was a very popular and profitable destination for shoppers. Despite the popularity of the York Road branch, Stewart's always found itself a distant fourth in terms of sales amongst Baltimore's department stores. This was especially true at its store at Howard and Lexington Streets. The store was usually seen as an "outsider" and "just didn't get Baltimore." That was especially the feeling of Governor Schaefer, who never thought much of Stewart's. "If you wanted to get the good stuff you went to Hutzler's. If you wanted to get ordinary stuff you went to Hochschild Kohn or the May Company," says Schaefer.

THE MAY COMPANY

Diagonally opposite Stewart's was the May Company, one of America's largest department store companies, which included the May Company name in Cleveland, Los Angeles and Denver. May's ties in Baltimore dated back

The downtown Stewart's as it appeared in 1980. The store closed its doors in January 1979. *Courtesy of Kevin A. Mueller.*

Originally built for Bernheimer-Leader Co., the May Company moved into this building in 1927. Hochschild Kohn is seen on the far right. The image was taken on January 24, 1944, during the effort to sell war bonds. *Courtesy of the Baltimore County Public Library Legacy Web.*

to 1927, when the company purchased the Bernheimer-Leader department store on Lexington Street.

In 1908, Bernheimer Bros. built another of Baltimore's "palaces," but it unfortunately was located on the less-traveled Fayette Street. The signature store with its limestone columns was designed to help shed its lower-end image. The store opened on March 9, 1908, to large crowds and much fanfare. But shoppers soon found themselves drawn back to Howard and Lexington Streets. Bernheimer needed a presence there and in 1923 purchased the small Leader Company department store. In 1925, Bernheimer-Leader built a massive eight-story emporium on the southwest corner of the fabled intersection. However, the company had overextended itself and went looking for a suitor. In 1927, May Company took over and reinvented the store to cater to the masses. In January 1941, plans were announced for an eight-story addition to its Lexington Street frontage, creating a store with 320,000 square feet of selling space.

In spite of a desire to expand, the May Company was never able to successfully develop suburban branches.

O'NEILL & CO.

"The only store that was more upscale than we [Hutzler's] was O'Neill's," says George Hutzler Bernstein. Thomas O'Neill came to Baltimore in 1866 and "made his fortune by founding and expanding a store that many considered to be the most prestigious emporium of its kind south of Wanamaker's in Philadelphia." In 1882, Thomas O'Neill opened his linen shop, which would eventually become the O'Neill & Co. department store.[20]

Thomas O'Neill will forever be remembered as the man who drove to the Carmelite Convent on Biddle Street and prayed with the nuns to help save his store during the great Baltimore fire of 1904. Just as the flames approached the building, firemen told O'Neill that they were going to blow up his store to stop the spread of fire. O'Neill stood in the doorway and refused to leave. He said that they would have to blow him up too. O'Neill eventually did leave and drove to the convent to pray. One story has it that he returned with holy water and sprinkled it on the building.[21] But for whatever reason, the wind shifted and his department store was saved. When he died in 1919, O'Neill left $7 million to the Archdiocese of Baltimore. That money largely helped fund the Cathedral of Mary Our Queen in 1959.[22]

O'Neill & Co. was purchased by Allied Stores in 1928. Over the years, the business was known as an old-fashioned store with unique detailed attention to personal customer service. The store had wooden floors and kept most of its merchandise behind wooden counters. Though O'Neill's had a frontage on Lexington Street, it was located on Charles Street, not Howard. After problems surfaced with the landlords and the threat of demolition from the soon-to-evolve Charles Center project, O'Neill's closed its doors on December 27, 1954. "When it was announced that O'Neill's was closing, people felt that the sky was falling," remembers columnist Jacques Kelly.

Several hundred employees were out of work when the store closed. Bob Eney said, "The designer person from O'Neill's moved to Hutzler's [after they closed] and all of the shopping elite came with her." So O'Neill's loss was Hutzler's gain, and this move helped Hutzler's sail even more steadily into the 1950s and 1960s. Soon the building that survived the great 1904 fire would succumb to the initial phase of Baltimore's new Charles Center project.

Gutman's

When columnist Jacques Kelly recalls downtown Baltimore, he feels that Baltimore was lucky to have five stores in its heyday. The fifth store that he cites is Julius Gutman Co., also known by locals as "JG's." Gutman's was a popularly priced department store founded in 1877. Kelly describes Gutman's as follows: "It was a wonderful department store of moderate prices and probably more racially mixed than the other stores. It was very busy and the first floor was a mad house. It was a big store, with elevators. It practiced the 'Wal-Mart business.' Gutman's would just carry things that the others wouldn't."

Gutman's eight-story Lexington Street store dated from 1928. The company expanded into the suburbs with small branches at Eastpoint and Harundale. In July 1959, Gutman's merged with another longtime popular priced store, Brager-Eisenberg. Brager's dated from 1882 and also branched out from downtown. The store consolidated its operations on Lexington Street and became Brager-Gutman's.

Another distant branch of the Gutman family comes to mind when one thinks of Baltimore retailing. That firm was Joel Gutman & Co. Not only was Joel Gutman & Co. notable for being Baltimore's first department store to open, it was also notable for being Baltimore's first department store to fail. Joel Gutman opened his dry goods store in 1852 but was also credited with opening Baltimore's first department store "palace." When Gutman opened his palace in November 1886, over three thousand people showed up at its grand opening. Two years later, in 1888, Hutzler opened its even more opulent palace. Located on Eutaw Street, Gutman was off of the high traffic intersection of Howard and Lexington Streets. As shopping patterns continued to change, Gutman's was forced to close its doors in 1929.[23] But the legacy of the Gutman family survived through the Hutzler family members. Department store co-founder David Hutzler married Ella Gutman in 1874. As mentioned before, the Baltimore department store scene did seem incestuous.

THE HECHT CO.

There is one more Baltimore retail family that must round out this chapter, and that is the Hecht family. Hecht's Reliable Store was founded on South Broadway in 1879. In 1885, the family added another store closer to the center of downtown named Hecht Bros., which provided home furnishings. Apparel was soon added into the merchandise mix. Successfully targeting the general population, the company continued to grow. A large store in the heart of Washington's downtown retail district at Seventh and F Streets was opened in 1896. One year later, efforts were refocused back on Baltimore, and within time Hecht became the company for everyone to watch.

In 1897, Hecht opened "its second most important store in the company," called the Hub, at Baltimore and Charles Streets. Once again, there was a commitment to merchandise of good quality and good price.[24] Though it was located far from "the Hub" of Howard and Lexington Streets, the Hub developed a very loyal following. "Baltimore had a lot of affection for 'the Hub,'" says columnist Jacques Kelly.

While successfully managing operations in both Baltimore and Washington, another Hecht Bros. store was opened on New York City's Fourteenth Street, a store the company operated until 1956. In 1947, Hecht began the march to the suburbs in Washington with the opening of a three-story branch in the far-flung community of Silver Spring, Maryland. Hecht realized that its future growth was in the suburbs, since it had been long shut out of Baltimore's main shopping intersection. Riding on the success of the Silver Spring branch, the Hecht Co. opened suburban stores in Baltimore—one in Northwood in 1955 and one in Edmondson in 1956, opposite the Hochschild Kohn store.

The whole playing field changed in October 1958 when the Hecht Co. announced a merger with the May Company. Finally the May Company got its suburban locations and finally Hecht had a location at Howard and Lexington Streets. It was the perfect match.[25] All Hecht operations were consolidated at the Howard Street store and Hecht-May was born. By 1962, it was all just simply the Hecht Co., and it soon was a force to be reckoned with.

THE RIGHT STORE, THE RIGHT PLACE, THE RIGHT TIME

Towson was a gold mine. Towson was fantastic. That's where the people lived. It was our customer.
—George Hutzler Bernstein,
vice-president and treasurer, 1960–82

After seeing the overwhelming success of Hochschild Kohn's two suburban stores, Hutzler's realized that it had to make a move. It didn't want to replace its Downtown store's flagship status. It was the "Main Store." However, Hutzler's customer base began to leave the city core, and across the country, the nationwide trek to suburbia began. Hutzler's identified its ideal customer as the Towson-Catonsville-Pikesville shopper and so the company focused its attention on Towson.[26]

In 1947, Hutzler's purchased land located right in the heart of Towson from Goucher College. The company focused all of its energy on developing the perfect suburban store. Once plans were designed and construction began, the company set a fall 1952 opening date. Former board member David Hutzler remembers, "The Towson store was a great effort. My father was the person in charge of the construction effort and having it come in on time. It was so nerve wracking to him that he actually came down with shingles."

Ground was broken for the Towson store on June 22, 1950. Hutzler's was building the "branch store of its dreams." The company proclaimed that the store would be large, modern and beautiful. Hutzler's Towson

A view of the windowless Towson Hutzler's as it nears completion. This image was taken in October 1952. The store would open for business one month later. *Courtesy of the Baltimore County Public Library Legacy Web.*

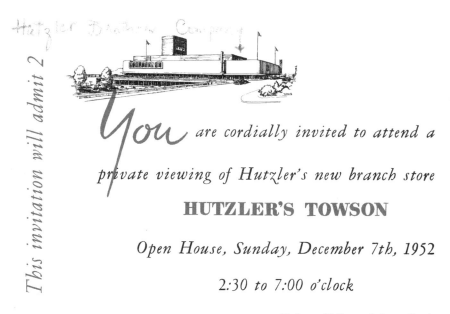

This invitation will admit 2

You are cordially invited to attend a private viewing of Hutzler's new branch store

HUTZLER'S TOWSON

Open House, Sunday, December 7th, 1952

2:30 to 7:00 o'clock

Dulaney Valley and Joppa Roads

An invitation to a private shopping night at the Towson Hutzler's on December 7, 1952. *Private collection.*

A view from the lower-level parking lot from December 1952 at the Towson Hutzler's. *Courtesy of the Baltimore County Public Library Legacy Web.*

The toy department on the upper level of the Towson store, circa 1953. *Courtesy of the Baltimore County Public Library Legacy Web.*

would "cater to the whole family in the traditional Hutzler fashion. It would bring Hutzler merchandise and service—and large scale parking, to the entire northern region of Metropolitan Baltimore."[27] Hutzler's chose Towson, the county seat of Baltimore County, as the ideal location for the company's first suburban store due to its convenient access to all of the surrounding suburban communities currently in the midst of a development boom. Little did the company know that this new store would quickly become the shopping destination not only for the Towson area, but practically all of Baltimore as well.

Hutzler's Towson opened for business on November 24, 1952. The store boasted that it was "designed chiefly to meet the requirements of the automobile age." Located at the intersection of Joppa Road and Dulaney Valley Road, the Towson Hutzler's main entrance directly fronted a one-thousand-car parking lot. The company also eliminated the usage of display windows in Towson. Instead, Hutzler's gave an overall view of the interior store with a continuous bank of windows. After two years of designing, the store planners decided that vehicular traffic would afford little or no time to gaze at the show windows.[28] But display windows or not, the Towson Hutzler's was a hit from day one.

The store's third floor was home to the Valley View Room, where diners overlooked the stunning view of Hampton Mansion. The restaurant, also referred to as the Tea Room, featured murals that were painted on canvas panels in "comfortable department store pastels." The murals included the Baltimore oriole, the black-eyed Susan, Timonium Fairgrounds and fox hunting, among other scenes. The people depicted in the murals were dressed in Edwardian costumes. Up until the late 1970s, the Valley View Room boasted its own bakery that featured Hutzler originals such as the Lady Baltimore cake, the Lord Baltimore cake—which contained chopped walnuts within the white marshmallow icing—and the Goucher Cake. Named after nearby Goucher College, the dessert was a white fluffy cake with mocha icing and crushed cashew nuts sprinkled on top. The Valley View Room also featured live fashion modeling and was the home of countless parties and other festivities.[29]

The store was conceived and planned on a much larger scale than any other previous suburban Baltimore store. As its popularity grew, so did the size of the store. Even at 159,000 square feet, Hutzler's was forced to add a new parking deck in 1963 and an entire new fourth floor in 1967.

It was obvious that Hutzler's real destiny was in the suburbs. The Howard Street location was still considered its home, but the store's future centered in

The lounge of the Valley View Room at the Towson Hutzler's, circa 1953. *Courtesy of the Baltimore County Public Library Legacy Web.*

One of the famous murals at the Valley View Room in Towson. This mural depicts Hampton Mansion. *Courtesy of the Baltimore County Public Library Legacy Web.*

A view of the lower-level entrance to Hutzler's in Towson, circa summer 1961. This entrance was built below Joppa Road. This is currently the site of the popular Trader Joe's market. *Courtesy of the Baltimore County Public Library Legacy Web.*

Towson. "I loved the Towson store because all of the key Hutzler people were there," says former employee Lynn Stecher Cox. Hutzler's Towson brought style, sophistication and new merchandise to the residents of Baltimore's growing northern suburbs. "For a while the Towson store got one copy of *Variety* every week. I used to get it. I was really young and I am amazed that they did get it, thinking back on it," states filmmaker John Waters.

As Towson grew, so did Hutzler's. Over time, the store became the highest-grossing department store in the Baltimore area. Just like the Downtown store, Hutzler's Towson served generations of customers. It was a recipe that was hard to repeat, and for many Baltimoreans, it was a store that was hard to let go.

THE SALE OF THE CENTURY

With the Towson store firmly established, Hutzler's felt secure with its place in Baltimore's retail environment. Some shoppers preferred the ease of Towson while others still preferred Downtown. The Art Deco beauty of the Howard Street store was enticing. Columnist Jacques Kelly was a "Downtown" person. "It was a cathedral, a beautifully designed building," says Kelly.

The Howard Street store defined the image of that era's Downtown department store. George Hutzler Bernstein states, "If you walked into that Saratoga Street entrance and looked across that balcony, it was a grand emporium." Going downtown in the 1950s was still the thing to do. Department stores always targeted their merchandise to women who would come and spend the entire day shopping, eating, browsing and relaxing.

A favorite pastime was a trip to Hutzler's and having a meal in one of its restaurants. The main dining room of the Downtown store was the Colonial Restaurant. Also referred to as the Tea Room, the Colonial dated back to 1917. By 1935, the restaurant was air conditioned. On December 10, 1942, the Colonial moved from the fourth floor into its new home on the sixth floor of the "New Building." On that first day, 1,053 people ate at the Colonial in a location that seated 262 diners. The store proclaimed that the new Colonial with its "glowing reds, restful blues and sense of spaciousness and ease put shoppers in a happy mood for meals and convalescence."[30]

In some ways, the reputation of the Colonial was even greater than that of the Downtown store. Eating at the Colonial was at least one part of a

A window display featuring Hutzler's housewares department from May 1950. *Courtesy of Jacques Kelly.*

Hutzler's new Teen Fashion Board is displayed in this store window in August 1951. *Courtesy of Jacques Kelly.*

A view of the basement store at the Downtown Hutzler's, circa 1950s. *Courtesy of Jacques Kelly.*

The Colonial Restaurant at the Downtown Hutzler's. *Gift of Jacques Kelly, courtesy of the Jewish Museum of Maryland, 2000.141.004.*

woman's day of shopping. Women dressed with hats, high heels and gloves for lunch and appeared as if they had a very important day of shopping ahead of them. Saturday was the day of choice for such an event, and shopping at Hutzler's and having lunch in the store's Tea Room was a sophisticated social activity for many female Hutzler customers.

But the Colonial also served a high-power male clientele as well. The restaurant's food, service, atmosphere and location made the Colonial a destination for Baltimore's businessmen. Governor William Donald Schaefer frequently ate at the Colonial Restaurant. "The big shots went to the Colonial Restaurant. I used to fake that I was a waiter just to get in," says Schaefer.

The Colonial was also known as the only restaurant in Baltimore that regularly served terrapin stew. Here was a restaurant where women could watch a fashion show while eating a sliced hard-cooked egg sandwich served on the store's signature cheese toast.

Also located on the sixth floor next door to the Colonial was the Quixie, a one low price restaurant where complete meals could be had for a dollar. The Quixie opened after the store's 1942 expansion and remained in operation until 1972. Young girls who were in vocational training staffed the Quixie. These girls, under the strict supervision of Mary B. Cooper,

The Quixie, with its distinctive tables and chairs at the Downtown Hutzler's. *Gift of Jacques Kelly, courtesy of the Jewish Museum of Maryland, 2000.141.001.*

Young girls in vocational training would deliver the food to the diners on carts. Note the traditional square-shaped Hutzler's cake. *Courtesy of Jacques Kelly.*

would have had a hard time gaining employment elsewhere, as they were "mentally challenged." About six different meals were offered daily for a fixed price. Desserts were extra. Upon entering the Quixie, the customer paid her bill in advance so that no cash would change hands. She was then handed a menu along with a pencil to check off the meal selection so the waitress would not have to write an order. A couple of hostesses helped "patrol" the restaurant.

The Colonial and the Quixie were sleek and modern, reminiscent of a 1930s movie set. These two restaurants set Hutzler's apart from the other downtown stores. When people thought of shopping and eating downtown, they thought of Hutzler's.[31] When people went to eat at Hutzler's, it was typically a very special event. Senator Barbara Mikulski remembers such visits to Hutzler's with her mother. She states, "I remember the wonderful Tea Room and the white-gloved women leading you to the elevators. I remember the chicken salad, and my mother telling me to sit up straight and act like a lady. I felt like I was in an Audrey Hepburn movie."

Seven floors below the Colonial and Quixie was the home of the basement luncheonette. The luncheonette served one of Baltimore's best chocolate sodas, which was accompanied by the rumble of the B&O railroad trains as they traveled through the downtown train tunnels. The luncheonette opened when the Downstairs Store opened in 1929 and was an Art Deco masterpiece. One of the most popular dishes served in the basement, and only the basement, was chicken chow mein. Legend had it that Asian people made the chicken chow mein in their own kitchens and wheeled it into the store in large tubs.[32] Many people preferred the counters and stools of the luncheonette to the other Hutzler restaurants.

Across Saratoga Street was the Fountain Shop, located next to the Rug Department. Designed in 1954 with the renovation of the Annex, it was a popular restaurant where people could watch their food travel through the restaurant on conveyor belts.

From the formal Colonial Restaurant to the Saratoga Street bakery with its square cakes, Hutzler's could handle all dining needs. Hutzler's not only clothed and employed Baltimoreans, but it also fed them. And in true Hutzler

The Fountain Shop was located across Saratoga Street in Hutzler's Annex. It was the scene of the store's first sit-in demonstration. *Courtesy of Jacques Kelly.*

A view of the main entrance of Hutzler's on Howard Street, circa 1957. *Courtesy of Jacques Kelly.*

tradition, the store did so with quality. "I did love the Hutzler food. It was delicious. Bar none, it was the best department store food that I ever tasted," says Jacques Kelly.

The Saratoga Street entrance was not home solely to Hutzler's famous bakery. It was also home to the store's famous message book. Here, customers could leave notes for one another that might read "Doris, meet me at the Colonial at 2." This service predated the cellular telephone days. Along with the message book on the Saratoga balcony entrance, Hutzler's had two large Art Moderne benches where people would meet, even when the store was mobbed. For many, the benches served a much greater purpose than the message book.

Hutzler's also practiced generous customer policies that included carfare home if the customer had forgotten her pocketbook. Charge customers would receive a sympathy note from the president or chairman of the board if a spouse passed away.[33]

In order to achieve maximum buying power, Hutzler's was a member of the Associated Merchandising Corporation. AMC was a store-owned buying company that allowed stores to pool their resources and buy goods in bulk. Along with stores such as Strawbridge & Clothier in Philadelphia

Above: The stylish "Bra Bar" located inside the Downtown store. The photo dates from November 1957. *Courtesy of Jacques Kelly.*

Opposite, top: The fabrics department located inside Hutzler's original 1888 Palace building, circa 1955. *Courtesy of Jacques Kelly.*

Opposite, bottom: Another view of the fabrics department at the Downtown store. *Courtesy of Jacques Kelly.*

and Thalhimers in Richmond, AMC served many of America's leading department stores. One such member of AMC was the J.L. Hudson Co. Hudson's was not only Detroit's largest store, but it was America's second-largest department store. George Hutzler Bernstein recalls the embarrassment of being at AMC meetings. Orders would be placed in alphabetical order of store name, and Hutzler's immediately followed Hudson's in the alphabet. "Hudson's would order one thousand dozen of some order and then Hutzler's would order two dozen. We were the pipsqueak in AMC," says Bernstein.

One unusual department at Hutzler's was the Bureau of Adjustments. "The name 'Bureau of Adjustments' was just a funny name for the

Above: Hutzler's famous shoe department at its Howard Street store, circa 1960. *Courtesy of Jacques Kelly*.

Below: The fifth-floor gift department at the Downtown Hutzler's, circa 1950s. *Courtesy of Jacques Kelly*.

Baltimore deejay Buddy Deane signs autographs in the fourth-floor teen department during the company's Centennial Exposition in 1958. *Courtesy of the Maryland Historical Society.*

Complaint Department," says George Hutzler Bernstein. If a salesperson or a supervisor did not satisfy a customer then the customer would be referred here. "What I usually would do is ask 'what would you like us to do?' Most of the time the customer would ask for less than the store was prepared to offer," says Bernstein.

Hutzler's employees, also known as Hutzlerites, appeared as one big, happy, loyal family. Hutzlerites felt like family because they were treated like family. This special feeling made them proud to be an employee of Hutzler's. Sue Gaston Sachs was a former buyer who knew what it felt like to be a member of the Hutzler family. Sachs says, "It was a terrific and fun place to work. The pay was not the best but the 'aura' of working for Hutzler's was more than enough. We all felt that we worked for the premier department store in Baltimore and we took pride in that." A total of 886 Hutzlerites lined up for the new polio vaccine in 1957.[34]

Store planning continued as executives searched for possible future suburban locations. By 1957, the first executives from outside of the Hutzler family, Edward Leavy as the vice-president of finance and

Above: Mary Lou Welschmyer of Corning Glass demonstrated how to cook using Pyrex cookware at the company's Centennial Exposition in 1958. *Courtesy of the Maryland Historical Society.*

Opposite, top: Large birthday cakes, along with a replica of Hutzler's first store, adorn the façade on Howard Street during the 100th anniversary celebration in 1958. *Courtesy of Jacques Kelly.*

Opposite, bottom: A woman shops for buttons at the Centennial Exposition downtown in 1958. *Courtesy of Jacques Kelly.*

Marian Merrick as general merchandising manager, came on board. Things began to change at Hutzler's. On January 1, 1958, Hutzler's began the year with a full-page advertisement in the *Baltimore Sun*: "We Light our 100th Candle."

Hutzler's spent the better part of the year celebrating its 100th anniversary. The Hutzler Centennial Exposition began on February 24 and lasted until March 1. The event included product demonstrations, special exhibits and visits by personalities. The Downtown store erected large birthday cakes on its exterior and even built a replica of the M. Hutzler & Son store on the

Where Baltimore Shops

exact same spot where the original store was located. Dan Sachs, a former merchandise manager, recalls,

> *The anniversary was a big deal that featured tons of decorations and promotions. Perhaps the greatest personal memory was the party for the employees at the Fifth Regiment Armory* [on April 12, 1958]. *Employees were encouraged to come in costume and the Hutzler family arrived at the party and was driven around in a horse-drawn carriage. Another employee, buyer Bill Hughlett, was a hit of the party when he arrived dressed as a Hutzler gift box.* [35]

The year's festivities helped cement Hutzler's as the premier store in Baltimore. The anniversary celebration culminated with the opening of another suburban store.

WE ARE NOT A TREE

Albert Hutzler Jr. could not stand the term "branch stores." Once at a meeting, Albert loudly declared, "We are not a tree!" Any location other than the Downtown store was always referred to as a "suburban" store.[36] With that in mind, Hutzler's was anxious to repeat the success of its Towson store. The company turned its sights to East Baltimore.

Hutzler's opened its second suburban store at the Eastpoint Shopping Center on October 10, 1956. Located at Eastern Avenue and North Point Road, it joined anchors Hochschild Kohn and Penn Fruit in a retail center designed to serve the working-class communities of Essex and Dundalk. The store originally sold only apparel goods, and from the first day, the store was a challenge. George Hutzler Bernstein says the following about the Eastpoint store: "Hutzler's had always been the top-quality image store. Eastpoint was in an industrial area. They tried to maintain that image in a blue-collar neighborhood. The management was dogmatic about keeping the image of the fine carriage trade store. That was, in my opinion, the beginning of the demise."

All members of the family did not necessarily share these sentiments. Richard Hutzler states, "Eastpoint was a challenge to my dad, who had conceived it as a branch of the Downstairs Store. We found that the public was offended by the merchandise that was offered. They wanted the good stuff, too. They didn't want to be limited to the Downstairs Store [type of merchandise]."

So a disagreement ensued about the merchandise mix at the Eastpoint store. What was obvious was the fact that Eastpoint was not the success

The Eastpoint Hutzler's store as seen in 1956. *Courtesy of the Baltimore County Public Library Legacy Web.*

that Towson was. What was also obvious was that the Hutzler family was splitting apart.

Regardless, the Eastpoint store was in it for the long haul. In August 1964, Hutzler's announced plans to enlarge the Eastpoint store by adding a third level. This additional floor space enabled more merchandise to be displayed, and a home furnishings department was added.[37]

The next store to open made a much bigger splash. As a culmination of its 100th anniversary celebration, Hutzler's Westview debuted on September 29, 1958. When it opened, the Westview store was the largest of the suburban stores, with 185,000 square feet of selling space. The store was located on Baltimore National Pike and predated the Baltimore Beltway by a couple of years. It had a gala opening, and the store capitalized on the success of West Baltimore locations that other retailers such as Hochschild's and Hecht Co. had. Hutzler's three-story Westview location also was home to the popular Maryland Gardens restaurant, known for its scenic murals.

In its earlier years, some swore that the Westview store, and not the Towson store, was a close second to Downtown.[38] Westview enjoyed success for many years and was later joined by Stewart's in the shopping center. Many people

Where Baltimore Shops

The Westview store's mall entrance on its opening day. *Courtesy of the Baltimore County Public Library Legacy Web.*

The Westview Hutzler's store, with its "space age" entrance, as seen on September 19, 1958. *Courtesy of the Baltimore County Public Library Legacy Web.*

The bridal department at the Westview Hutzler's store. *Courtesy of the Baltimore County Public Library Legacy Web.*

began their careers at Hutzler's by starting first at the Westview store. But as West Baltimore began to have troubles, the area around Westview was also impacted.[39] "With Westview, it was the area that failed. Westview never really did make the mark that it was supposed to make," says former employee Lynn Stecher Cox. Hutzler's learned that it was going to be impossible to replicate the success of the Towson store. "Westview wasn't like Towson. It just didn't come off as well," says Mrs. Albert D. "Bunny" Hutzler Jr.

Nonetheless, Westview was still one of Hutzler's signature stores with its space-age canopy and its loyal customer following. It never quite lived up to the success of Towson, as some of its ardent supporters believed, but it was still a store that the Hutzler family was proud of.

When Hutzler's announced plans in 1964 to enlarge its Eastpoint store, it also announced plans to open a store in Anne Arundel County. Hutzler's Southdale completed the suburban store circle around Baltimore. Southdale was unusual because it was located in a previously occupied building. Giant

Food had tried its luck in hard goods with a store at Ritchie Highway and Mountain Road. After Giant failed, Hutzler's took over the lease and opened its newest branch in the sprawling one-story structure on October 14, 1965. The company hoped that its location would appeal to shoppers from Annapolis and the Eastern Shore. The store featured the Chesapeake Bay Room restaurant, with its photo mural of log canoes by the noted photographer A. Aubrey Bodine. Eventually, the store added a floor-to-ceiling clock near the Men's and Boys' Department, and the store took on the expression, "Meet me at the clock."[40]

The Southdale store also missed the mark when it came to duplicating Towson's success. "Southdale was okay, not great," says Albert D. "Jiggs" Hutzler Jr. Other family members felt even stronger. "We put this store in Southdale and that was never a successful store. It was laid out on one floor. It was a strange duck. I think they got it at a great price," states George Hutzler Bernstein.

There is one more Hutzler building that is noteworthy. Hutzlerites "affectionately" called it "No. 10." This was the reference to Hutzler's Service Building—the term "warehouse" was not acceptable. Named after a number that was left on the chimney by its previous tenant, the Service Building was

A nighttime view of the Southdale Hutzler's on June 15, 1966. The store was located at Ritchie Highway and Mountain Road in Anne Arundel County. *Courtesy of the BGE collection at the Baltimore Museum of Industry.*

located at 719 West Lombard Street, near the downtown campus of the University of Maryland.[41] The building was purchased in 1946 and was later expanded to 100,000 square feet. All merchandise arrived at No. 10 and was subsequently checked in and marked for each store. It was then placed on trailers and shipped to individual stores.

The Service Building was located several blocks from the Downtown store. A shuttle bus would help the employees travel from one location to the other. A trip to the Service Building was usually a trip full of hard, tedious work. "No. 10 was the bane of every assistant buyer. All of the 'debits' were accumulated there, and assistants had to go regularly to sort them out and write for return labels to clear them out. It was a never-ending battle!" says buyer Sue Gaston Sachs.

By 1965, Hutzler's was a five-store company that served the complete metropolitan area of Baltimore. As noted, not all of its new locations were as successful as originally hoped. The Southdale store was the last location that Hutzler's opened for almost a decade. Some family members and employees began to question and challenge some of the company's business decisions. There was dissent in the Hutzler family. Downtown Baltimore was not only showing its age but was also about to experience a social revolution. Hutzler's kept a smile on its face and threw elaborate events in order to ensure itself as Baltimore's leading department store.

OCCASION EXTRAORDINAIRE

OE was truly an event and nothing in today's retail can compare. The line to get into the store was huge and it was pure mayhem when the doors were opened. It was truly the advent of the word "doorbuster"!
—*Sue Gaston Sachs, buyer, 1969–85*

Every year, Hutzler's hosted two major sales. Each April, the store held its Anniversary Sale, when many items in the store's stock were sold at least 20 percent off. But it was in October when many Baltimoreans enjoyed the biggest and most unusual sale of the year, the famous Hutzler's Occasion Extraordinaire.

Occasion Extraordinaire, also known as "OE," was very different from other stores' sales. For OE, buyers had to find desirable merchandise many months before the sale, often from Hutzler's import programs. Merchandise managers from every division reviewed the selected merchandise, and items were chosen based on value, desirability and availability. Then the buyers and merchandise managers went before the "Hard-boiled Committee" to present their selections for approval. Each item was inspected, and stringent rules had to be followed for pricing. All items had to be offered at a minimum of 20 percent off the regular retail price. A certain quantity had to be sold at regular price in order for it to qualify for a "sale" price in OE.[42]

If a selected item had been in the store's stock for at least two to three months, then the item could be sold for less. If a buyer wanted to sell an item at OE and it was not part of Hutzler's house stock, comparison shoppers

FRIDAY, OCTOBER 18th, WILL BE COURTESY DAY IN

THE FAMOUS HUTZLER Occasion Extraordinaire

A MARYLAND tradition is "The Hutzler Occasion Extraordinaire" — an event that's known throughout the state as our greatest sale of the year! As usual, you'll find hundreds of remarkable values throughout both the Main Store and Hutzler's Downstairs in this eagerly awaited event!

All items to be Advertised on Friday evening and Saturday morning will be AVAILABLE to you on FRIDAY

Save Time! Use Your Charga-Plate

A Maryland Institution
1858 1940

Occasion Extraordinaire

HUTZLER'S BULLETIN

Thursday, April 25, 1974

Management is pleased to announce to all employees that a sixth Hutzler store will open in Salisbury, Maryland.

The new 50,000 square foot store is scheduled to open in the Salisbury Mall in the spring of 1975. This mall, which opened in 1968, contains a Hecht store and a Sears store along with a number of specialty and service stores.

We look forward to serving the residents of the Delmarva Peninsula.

* * * * * * * * * * *

HUTZLER'S **116**th **anniversary sale**
every sale item is at least 20% off the price for which we would normally sell it

... OUR CELEBRATION OF 116 YEARS AS A MARYLAND INSTITUTION ... BEGINNING TODAY WITH COURTESY DAYS TODAY AND TOMORROW ... THEN CONTINUING INTO NEXT WEEK ...

Top: A postcard that announced the 1940 Occasion Extraordinaire. *Private collection.*

Middle: An Occasion Extraordinaire advertisement from October 1973. *Courtesy of Dan and Sue Sachs.*

Left: An advertisement for Hutzler's 116th Anniversary Sale from April 1974. *Courtesy of Dan and Sue Sachs.*

would have to locate the item at another place. Hutzler customers knew that they were getting a real value for a quality product.

For Executive Dan Sachs, OE was "sacred. Sacred in every way. People would line up at the doors like you would never have believed. They thought we were giving it away and in some ways we were." The Occasion sale was the unofficial kickoff to the Christmas season, even though it was in October. Customers in the know made many early Christmas purchases at OE time.

OE dated from before the 1930s, but the sale came to a halt in 1941 with the advent of World War II. In 1959, Hutzler's resurrected its "Greatest Sale of the Year."[43] There were two courtesy days for charge account shoppers as a special feature of both OE and the Anniversary Sale. Sue Gaston Sachs remembers,

> *My first OE was in Towson and it was unbelievable. The line to get into the store on the first of two "courtesy days" was huge. It was pure mayhem when the doors opened, truly the advent of the word "doorbuster." From the view on the selling floor it was one non-ending line to the register. OE was truly an event and nothing in today's retail can compare.*

Occasion Extraordinaire was a real Baltimore tradition, and it was an "Occasion" that the store celebrated until its final years.

Not only was Hutzler's known for its two sales, but it was also known for its festivals. Hutzler's festivals showcased exclusive European merchandise and helped maintain its image as the premier retail store of Baltimore. These events were held at a time when cities across the country were finding their core residential population shifting to the suburbs. With the exodus of middle-class residents, retailers in these cities found their customer base leaving as well. In some cities, department stores' sales began to decline as early as the middle of the 1950s. In Baltimore, stores held their own as the city entered the 1960s. Downtown was still the place to be, and Hutzler's enticed customers with its elaborate festivals in the Downtown store as well as in its suburban locations.

The first such festival, Festa Italiana, occurred in 1963. Led by Charles G. Hutzler III, Festa Italiana was the result of multiple buying trips all over Italy. On September 30, 1963, Hutzler's opened its one-week festival with members of the Italian Embassy as well as members of the Italian Ministry of Trade in attendance. The store proudly displayed Italian flags and fleur-de-lis throughout its store, but most importantly, the store exhibited for sale "the most desirable of Italian wares." The store also employed the head chef

The main floor of the Howard Street store is decorated with flags for the 1963 Festa Italiana. *Courtesy of the Maryland Historical Society.*

of Alitalia Airlines, who designed specific meals for each day of the week. The meals were served throughout the store's four restaurants. On a lesser scale, the Towson and Westview stores featured fine Italian merchandise along with demonstrations of glass blowing, leather tooling and woodcarving.[44]

In 1964, Hutzler's presented its Festival of Elegance. Hutzler buyers searched Western Europe for the "most elegant and designer wares from the fabled sights of Europe." The store featured Old World cuisine in its restaurants while the store was decorated in red, magenta and gold. One year later, in 1965, Hutzler's brought Fiesta Mexicana to the Baltimore shopping public.

Building on the success of Festa Italiana in 1963, Hutzler's planned Festa Italiana II. It opened on October 24, 1966, as a two-week festival that featured the fashions of five Italian designers. The store coordinated the festival with the Ministry of Foreign Trade. As a community service, Hutzler's ended Festa Italiana II with a gala benefit for the Baltimore Museum of Art.

A woman shops in the gift department during the 1963 Festa Italiana. *Courtesy of Jacques Kelly.*

Hutzler's was the store where many iconic items, such as Lego sets, Barbie dolls and Chatty Cathy dolls, debuted to the Baltimore public. When the store first put Barbie dolls on sale, the supply sold out within two hours. Hutzler's was famous for its Robert Bruce sweaters, which came in thirty different colors and four different sizes. It was clear that when people wanted to shop for something special, they went to Hutzler's first.[45]

Hutzler's was no stranger to television. It was the first business to demonstrate the invention to the city of Baltimore in 1947. By the 1960s, Hutzler's had staged several half-hour fashion shows on television. In 1967, the store presented the *Hutzler's Fashion Extravaganza* on WBAL-TV. The show featured the fall collection of featured designer Bill Blass. The title of the show was "The Rise and Fall of the Hemline as Seen through the Eyes of One Perplexed Male." The ratings of the show were excellent, and reviews of the program stated, "The models were utterly swish in the avant garde fashions."

Above: The china department helps promote Hutzler's 1964 Festival of Elegance. *Courtesy of the Jewish Museum of Maryland, 1995.169.012.*

Below: Another one of Hutzler's popular festivals was the Fiesta Mexicana at the Downtown Hutzler's store. *Courtesy of Jacques Kelly.*

Where Baltimore Shops

All through the mid-1960s, Hutzler's Downtown sustained its reputation as a leading shopping destination. The store still featured special touches such as finger bowls in the Colonial Room, the "real Santa," personalized chocolate Easter rabbits and special chocolate-covered strawberries for Mother's Day. Little touches like the "Fill the Sock Shop" for children—followed by the Sugar Plum Shop, where children could do their own Christmas shopping—made Hutzler's special.[46] Hutzler's Towson and Westview branches reported very strong sales. The business was in good shape.

A GIFT FROM HUTZLER'S
MEANS MORE

It was the place to be during the holidays, bustling with families in long coats and scarves to marvel at the fascinating, storytelling windows. Who needed Macy's windows in New York? We had Hutzler's!
—Senator Barbara Mikulski (D), Maryland

Soon after Occasion Extraordinaire ended in October, Hutzler's prepared for the Christmas season. Similar to other major cities, people in Baltimore were drawn to downtown at Christmastime. Howard and Lexington Streets was the retail hub for the region, and all of the stores were decked out with brilliant decorations and festive holiday windows. Santa Claus was downtown and was stationed in all of the large downtown stores. But everyone knew that the real Santa Claus was at Hutzler's.

All of the Hutzler stores celebrated the Christmas season in full decoration. Each of the original suburban Hutzler stores had its own Santa Claus. Each store carried a full array of toys. But the Downtown Hutzler's was famous for its windows. The Howard Street windows would change themes from year to year and always were animated.

When the new Towson branch store opened its doors for the first time in November 1952, customers entered a new store in the midst of its first Christmas season. Santa Claus was ready, seated on his throne, and children waited in line to tell him their wishes. The store was prepared for the Christmas rush with "attractive young girls garbed in Christmas red with holly wreathes in their hair." They acted as hostesses and greeted customers

Left: An early view of the Christmas gift wrapping department, circa 1940s. *Courtesy of Jacques Kelly*.

Below: The Howard Street store is decorated as "Presentville" for Christmas 1958. *Courtesy of Jacques Kelly*.

with welcome folders at each of the store's five entrances.[47] For years, the Towson store displayed a large Christmas tree on its roof. At the Westview, a two-ton Santa Claus was perched high atop that store.

Each Hutzler's store restaurant hosted Breakfast with Santa, a Christmas tradition. Santa would go from table to table, have his picture taken with the children and then listen to the children read their Christmas wish lists to him. It was a treasured event for the family. Baltimore County councilman Sam Moxley was a former Santa Claus for the Hutzler's at Westview in the late 1970s. Moxley had been working as the Santa in the Westview Mall and one day got a call from Molly Keach, director of personnel at Hutzler's Westview. "She said she needed a Santa tomorrow for a breakfast and I said that I could help out. That continued for a couple of weekends and then for a couple of years." After the breakfast, Santa would walk around the store greeting people. "The escalator bank at Westview was a real good place to give a big 'Ho, Ho, Ho,'" says Moxley.

Bernice Stein, the former Mrs. Albert D. Hutzler Jr., loved shopping at the Downtown store and helping people purchase their Christmas presents. "A friend of mine called and asked me to go down to the store and help him

The "Trim the Home" shop is featured near one of the store's fallout shelter areas during Christmas 1958. *Courtesy of Jacques Kelly.*

A view off the Saratoga Street balcony of Hutzler's main floor during Christmas 1958. *Courtesy of the Maryland Historical Society.*

The famous Christmas tree rests on the roof of the Towson Hutzler's store during Christmas 1960. *Courtesy of the Baltimore County Public Library Legacy Web.*

The Towson store is decorated with lights and snow on January 4, 1961. *Courtesy of the Baltimore County Public Library Legacy Web.*

The famous rooftop Santa Claus was an annual tradition at the Westview Hutzler's, circa 1950s. *Courtesy of the Baltimore County Public Library Legacy Web.*

pick out something for his wife for Christmas. I picked out two suits from the Dress Salon. After Christmas, his wife called me and was mad. She wanted a mink coat!" says Stein.

"A Gift from Hutzler's Means More" was the store's slogan for many years. It was a sign of prestige to receive a gift in a Hutzler's box. The store was known for its sturdy boxes, which were not constructed from flimsy cardboard. In many instances, people would place any purchase in a Hutzler's box. After Christmas, gift receivers went to Hutzler's in search of an exchange or a refund. They were not aware that their gift had not been purchased at Hutzler's, but the company accepted the merchandise anyway. "Albert Sr. always said that we should not argue with customers. Do whatever you need to do and over time it'll all pay off," says former executive Dan Sachs. He was right. Hutzler's shoppers were extremely loyal to their store, and the items that were not originally purchased at Hutzler's were usually given to charity.[48]

Hutzler's also was known for its "Men's Nights" during the Christmas season, when the doors were opened exclusively to male shoppers. The store was open only for the evening and it featured free drinks and hors d'oeuvres, in addition to live modeling. It was a tradition that continued for a number of years.[49] The stores would pull out all of the stops for Men's

A young child enjoys the Christmas windows at the Howard Street Hutzler's during Christmas 1971. *Courtesy of Jacques Kelly.*

Night, especially the Towson location. "It was a fun night, but for some men it was a 'knock down, drag out' evening. People do stupid things when they're drunk. Many men bought things that they couldn't afford," says former executive John Godfrey.

Hochschild's always gave Hutzler's a run for its money when it came to Christmastime. Hochschild's was famous for its Toytown parade. The Toytown parade was first held in 1936, and by 1964 it was viewed by over 250,000 people. It lasted until the late 1960s, when its floats and balloons began to show their wear and tear. The route of this Thanksgiving parade began near the Baltimore Museum of Art and eventually made its way down Howard Street, traveling right past Hutzler's front doors. When Santa arrived on his float at the end of the parade, he would walk right into Hochschild's main doors. But that didn't concern most Baltimoreans—everybody knew that Hutzler's had the real Santa Claus, because Hutzler's was "the only store."

THE BEST OF EVERYTHING

Hutzler's employees knew they were the best and they thought they were the best.
They lived up to their reputation. They took such pride in that place.
—Gilbert Sandler, Baltimore historian

It was hard to determine what exactly set Hutzler's apart from the other large stores on Howard Street. The store was known throughout Baltimore for carrying the best of everything. Its Downstairs Store helped fulfill the needs of some of its clientele, while the upstairs departments catered to those in search of the finest quality goods. Hutzler's had the élan, or the panache, because it was uncompromising in getting top-of-the-line merchandise.[50]

In the Men's Department, Hutzler's carried a line called Oxxford. It was very expensive, and of course, it was exclusively at Hutzler's. "They made themselves the gold standard of quality merchandise in Baltimore," states Baltimore historian Gilbert Sandler. This was true of the other departments in the store. Whether it was women's clothing or furniture, the store carried the best. Manufacturers knew that the best quality outlet in Baltimore was Hutzler's.

Hutzler's buyers traveled the world in search of superior merchandise. It was not unusual for a buyer to make frequent trips to Italy or the Orient in search of unique goods to sell. Hutzler's buyers were entrusted to find the finest merchandise. Their "taste buds for fashion" had to be sharp. If the goods weren't "the best," they were at least unique. In the 1960s, Hutzler's sold some of the first topless bathing suits for women in the country. "Some

Shopping for hats at the downtown Hochschild Kohn store. *Courtesy of Jacques Kelly.*

of our best customers came from Baltimore Street for the designer swimwear. Blaze Starr [one of Baltimore's most colorful exotic dancers] was one of our best customers in that department. A lot of women from 'the Block' shopped there as well," says former executive Nancy Thorn.

Customers would shop in the store's many salons, including the Rose Room, in search of quality fashions. Hutzler's made it its business to get the big names and to hold onto them. Although O'Neill's and Stewart's were competitive, also carrying fine merchandise and offering personal service, neither store could match the allure of Hutzler's.[51]

The store trusted and believed in its employees, resulting in fine merchandise and exceptional service. "Hutzler's cared about their customers, they cared about their employees and they cared about learning their employees' names as much as they could," says Nancy Thorn. Hutzler employees were proud to be Hutzlerites because they knew that their store was unsurpassed.

The trust and respect continued behind the scenes. "As long as you had good reasoning behind a business decision, they trusted you," says Thorn. Buyers not only had to learn what merchandise was available around the world, but they also had to learn how to market and stock each of the company's stores.

Hutzler's executives traveled to all of the stores on a regular basis. The executives tried to visit each store at least once a month. It was tricky to do business in Baltimore because the city was so polarized with its different sections. Eastpoint bought differently from Towson, and Westview was different from Eastpoint. Each store had its own identity, and it was imperative that each buyer understood the demographics surrounding each store. Executive Nancy Thorn stated:

> Towson was "horse country," "country club" and classic clothing. It was our best store and its customers had the highest income. Towson had the finest taste and the most "couture" taste. At Eastpoint, you couldn't sell anything if it didn't have a union label in it. It was such a "union" part of the city. I never knew why we sold so much black clothing at Eastpoint? I later learned, after making friends with department managers out there, that there were so many different ethnic groups out there and each one had its own funeral parlor. Westview was a little glitzy. Blue sold very well at Westview, don't ask me why. Westview wasn't about money. There was money out there at Westview but they didn't necessarily spend it on clothes. Southdale was coming up on Towson in taste. The same merchandise at Towson appealed to the customers at Southdale, but their taste was not as expensive. Downtown was a strange mixture. The store did a good designer business into the late 1970s. After a while, the clientele kind of changed.

It was clear that Hutzler's buyers knew their different markets throughout Baltimore, and that understanding helped the company enjoy success well into the 1970s.

SOCIETY PAGE

In the riots in Baltimore, nobody wanted to burn Hutzler's. I never felt that
Hutzler's was the enemy.
—*John Waters, Baltimore filmmaker*

Hutzler's was a huge account for the *Baltimore Sun* newspaper. Traditionally, department stores were the largest advertisers in local newspapers. In Baltimore, Hutzler's was not the only large account. The Hecht Co., Hochschild's and Stewart's all ran frequent large-scale newspaper advertisements in not only the *Baltimore Sun* but also the *Evening Sun* and the *Baltimore News American*. However, Hutzler's held ownership of the premier page of the city's largest newspaper.

In every Sunday *Baltimore Sun* newspaper, readers opened the Society page and saw that the entire front page was an advertisement for Hutzler's. It wasn't a sale ad or a clearance ad; it was a first-class advertisement of the latest fashion offering.[52] Buyer Sue Sachs remembers the newspaper ads from the front page of the Sunday Society section. "These fashion leader ads were always something special." All of the ads were done in house by a staff of talented artists. Hutzler's Society page advertisements usually were sketched and commanded attention. In addition, Hutzler's owned the back page of the News section from the *Morning Sun* from Monday through Saturday. However, the daily prize for Hutzler's was a quarter-size ad run every Monday through Friday on page 3. Merchandise managers and buyers wanted their respective department's goods to be featured in that ad. "We would fight amongst ourselves for that space. The merchandise managers and buyers wanted that ad more than anything else," says former executive Dan Sachs. Huge scrapbooks of all of the advertisements and resulting sales were kept for future reference.[53]

Hutzler's was determined to always keep its position as a high-image store. However, being a high-image store didn't necessarily mean high profits. "There was never a time when we made profits comparable to what we should have been making," says George Hutzler Bernstein. Members of the Hutzler family began to fight about which direction the company should go. Some wanted change. Hutzler's soon found that society would dictate the change.

Baltimore, and Maryland in general, had always played a pivotal role regarding the segregation between blacks and whites. Though the importation of slaves was deemed illegal in 1808, Baltimore still actively participated in domestic slave trade up until the Civil War. Baltimore also had the largest concentration of free blacks in the country because of its early involvement in trade with the West Indies. When the Civil War erupted, the first casualties of the war occurred in the city of Baltimore. Fighting broke out on Pratt Street when troops moved across town between the railroad depots. Baltimore was viewed as a battleground between Northern and Southern loyalties.[54]

Baltimore was considered the northernmost boundary of the integration social movement. Blacks tried to integrate public commercial facilities through peaceful sit-in demonstrations. Beginning in 1955, students from nearby Morgan State targeted the segregated facilities at the nearby Northwood Theatre and Read's Drug Store for protest demonstrations. On March 16, 1960, students targeted the restaurant at the Hecht-May store in Northwood. After the store refused service, Hecht-May sought a court injunction blocking further demonstrations. [55]

The students then set their sights on the downtown department stores. Hochschild Kohn was targeted, specifically in reaction to its policy of marking all merchandise sold to black customers "Final Sale." Black customers were also not allowed to try on intimate apparel or hats. In a letter to Issac Kohn, customer Madeline W. Murphy expressed outrage over the assumption that "Negroes are not bodily clean, have some sort of disease or that their hair is objectionable to the point of being unsanitary." Many black customers ended up traveling to Philadelphia or New York to do their shopping, where segregation was not widely practiced in the retail stores.

Rationalizing southern sensibilities, customers feared close physical contact with blacks, especially at lunch counters. In March 1960, protesters entered the four department stores determined to be served in the stores'

Left: The January 5, 1958 Sunday *Baltimore Sun* Society page features an advertisement about Hutzler's Centennial Sale. *Courtesy of Jacques Kelly.*

Below: The Northwood Hecht Co. store, as seen on January 21, 1955, was the scene of Baltimore's first sit-in demonstration. *Courtesy of the Baltimore County Public Library Legacy Web.*

restaurants. Students were either turned away or seated but not served. They reacted by setting up pickets at the entrances to the stores, and over the next days and weeks, sales began to slide. Protesters even made their way up to Hutzler's sixth floor as they marched around the lounge in a peaceful manner. By April, Hochschild Kohn boldly abandoned its restaurant's segregation policy.[56]

Protesters next focused their energy on Hutzler's Fountain Shop, located in Hutzler's Annex. It was a restaurant that stressed convenience and was a place where customers could grab a quick lunch. Black employees waited on customers, but there was an unwritten rule that service was unavailable to blacks. On a fateful April day, blacks entered the Fountain Shop and demanded service. The manager panicked, and tensions in the restaurant grew. The executive office was called and the manager was able to reach both Albert Sr. and Albert Jr. The manager asked, "What do we do?" Albert Sr. replied, "Serve them." Jiggs Hutzler, Albert Jr.'s son, feels that the Hutzler family wanted to "serve them long ago. But it was different times."

Hochschild's, Hutzler's, Stewart's and Hecht-May banded together and opened their dining facilities to all. The decision didn't come without customer backlash. Some white customers took their business out of town and closed longtime charge accounts. Longtime Baltimore resident and historian Gilbert Sandler recalls, "These were years of stress and strain because the leadership of the department stores knew it was the right thing to do. They were worried about business. Integration was a hard thing to do because many customers resisted it."

By the middle of the 1960s, increasing racial tensions in Baltimore sparked residential flight to the suburbs. Many white middle-class families left the city and settled in the suburbs surrounding Baltimore. As middle-class residents moved away, many retail and commercial establishments followed. This brought sharp sales declines to businesses in both downtown and neighborhood locations.

On April 4, 1968, Reverend Martin Luther King Jr. was assassinated in Memphis, Tennessee. Within two days, rioting broke out in over one hundred cities across the United States, including Baltimore. Cars were seen driving through the neighborhoods of East and West Baltimore hurling firebombs into small businesses. Soon afterward, businesses were looted before they were destroyed by fire. Corner stores were easy targets, especially in Jewish neighborhoods. Businesses along Gay Street were heavily destroyed. The National Guard was called and the city braced for more damage. "I remember

A neighborhood grocery store is looted on April 4, 1968, during the riots that hit Baltimore and other major American cities. *Courtesy of the Maryland State Police.*

being up on the roof of the store and I could just see smoke coming out of many different locations," says Jiggs Hutzler. The riots changed the history of the city. Downtown was protected fairly well by the National Guard, but the outlying areas were in danger. West Baltimore was on fire for a month. The fear of destruction spread into Baltimore's suburbs. Even the Towson Hutzler's, the pride of the company, had its first-floor windows bricked over in order to prevent any possible damage.[57] After two weeks of disturbance, the city calmed. The riots forever changed the perception of living, working and shopping in the city of Baltimore.

Although they escaped physical damage, Baltimore's department stores were financially hammered by the riots. Within two years, business at the Downtown Hutzler's declined 50 percent. Department stores were "real estate rich," but after the riots real estate values plummeted 50 to 80 percent. The main floor of the Downtown store, once bustling with shoppers, became eerily quiet almost overnight.[58]

By the end of the 1960s, it was plain as day that the social climate had changed. "The riots of '68 were a large turning point for downtown," says George Hutzler Bernstein. In addition to the riots, the United States was embroiled in the controversial Vietnam War and the "hippie era" had begun. Young people turned their backs on the Establishment, and that included department stores. Department stores were viewed as places where grandmothers shopped, and many young people were not interested in serving on "teen boards" or wearing designer sweaters.

Family roles began to change. The sole breadwinner concept faded as two working spouses supported more and more families. Time was precious. People found they just didn't have the time or desire to go downtown for an afternoon. It was no longer a social event. "The old carriage trade shoppers were women in white gloves that went downtown and had the time to do it. They weren't working back then," says Albert D. Hutzler III. It was the beginning of the end of the carriage-trade retailer.[59]

The 1970s brought about a major retailing revolution. Shopping centers continued to open in the suburbs and people continued to flee the inner city. Discounters like E.J. Korvette and Luskin's challenged department store pricing. Hutzler's needed guidance and leadership, but family infighting stood in its way.

FAMILY BUSINESS

If you have a business that doesn't change, somebody will run right by you.
The Hecht Co. ran right by us.
—*George Hutzler Bernstein, vice-president and treasurer, 1960–82*

F or the most part, the optimism of the 1950s and 1960s had disappeared by 1970. The company hadn't opened a suburban store since 1965. Just as quickly as sales declined at its Downtown store, theft was on the rise. In the March 1971 issue of the in-house magazine, *Tips and Taps*, Hutzler's published a large article on "The Staggering Costs of Employee Dishonesty." The article described how employee theft was increasing at an alarming rate and that each stolen $10 bill cost the store $300 in profits. The company stressed the importance of calling store security when theft was suspected.

The following *Tips and Taps* issue was titled "What Happens When You Dial 234?" Dialing 234 on an in-house phone directly connected to Hutzler's Security Control Center as it looked for "suspected shoplifters or rowdyism." Gone were the articles about employee picnics and in-store festivals. Hutzler's tried to update its merchandising display techniques by adding more racks for hanging but also warned salespeople to be on the lookout for increased shoplifting, as the new setup made merchandise easier to steal. Hutzler's found itself doing whatever it could to avoid further loss of merchandise or profit.[60]

Hutzler's was the last remaining family-run department store, but it was also one of the few independent department stores left in the country. In

A street view of Howard Street from June 14, 1973, showing all four major department stores. *Courtesy of the BGE collection at the Baltimore Museum of Industry.*

The Budget Store at the Westview store from 1970. *Courtesy of the Jewish Museum of Maryland, 1995.169.127.*

1958, the Hecht Co. became part of the May Department Stores Company. In 1960, Stewart's became a division of Associated Dry Goods. In 1969, Hochschild Kohn became part of Supermarkets General, the operator of Howland's, Steinbach, Pathmark grocery stores and Rickel's Home Centers. All of these companies provided financial support to their stores. Without the financial backing of a national holding company, Hutzler's was faced with severe financial hurdles in order to achieve growth and build inventory. "It was obvious that we didn't make any money. We didn't make any appreciative amount of profit, and without profit you can't expand reasonably," says George Hutzler Bernstein.

As part of the May Company, the Hecht Co. was able to expand and upgrade. Inventory was appropriately chosen to match the demographics of its store locations, whether it was Northwood or Golden Ring. As Hecht was doing a better merchandising job, it was also doing a better marketing job.[61] This was in stark contrast to Hutzler's merchandising decisions, which continued to target the upscale customer regardless of individual locations' demographics. "Hutzler's was marketing to the elite while the Hecht Co. was marketing to the general public," says Bernstein.

It took money to make money, and selling chic merchandise required even more capital. In order to be at the top of the pyramid, Hutzler's had to find a suitor. In 1972, it thought it had one. On July 17, 1972, President Albert D. Hutzler Jr., the third generation of the firm, surprised many of his employees by issuing the following letter and press release:

To all Hutzlerites:

Hutzler Brothers Company, an historic Baltimore retail department store organization, will be acquired by AMFAC, Inc., when final approval is given to terms of a tentative agreement.

Under terms of the proposed agreement, AMFAC common stock will be exchanged for all common stock of Hutzler Brothers Company. This transaction is subject to approval of the Board of Directors of AMFAC and the Board of Directors of Hutzler's. It is anticipated that the transaction will be closed by September 15, 1972.

"We long have looked toward the Eastern seaboard as a logical extension of our growing retail interests," Henry A. Walker, President of AMFAC said. In addition to the Joseph Magnin specialty stores noted for their fashion leadership, AMFAC operates the high quality and fashion-conscious Liberty House stores in Hawaii and California, including the famed City

of Paris by Liberty House in San Francisco: the Rhodes Department Stores along the Pacific Coast and in the Southwest: and the Rhodesway mass merchandising stores in California.

"Throughout its long history in Baltimore, Hutzler's has developed a reputation for fashion, quality and service," Albert D. Hutzler, Jr. said. "And AMFAC, for almost 123 years, has built its reputation on the same concept. We are confident the merging of these two fine retail organizations will be of benefit to both companies. Most importantly, to the employees and customers of Hutzler's—the people who have made possible our success as merchandisers to many generations of Maryland citizens."

Albert D. Hutzler Jr. went on to say that many important retailing organizations had sought to acquire the family-owned business over the years. He also stressed that the Hutzler family would remain an integral part of the Hutzler's business, with the present officers continuing in their respective responsibilities. At the time of the AMFAC merger, Hutzler's five stores totaled 1,200,000 square feet of space and employed over four thousand workers. The merger forecasted a new large store in Northwest Baltimore in 1975 and another large store in Northeast Baltimore in 1979. Hutzler's finally had the backing of a nationwide concern, and pending approval from both organizations' boards, the store would be able to look to the future with confidence and security.

For reasons undisclosed, the merger was canceled and the branch store expansion plans were put on hold. Employees were confused as to why the deal fell through. The store was back to business as usual. In *Tips and Taps*, Hutzler's made little note of the AMFAC deal and instead featured an article entitled "TV monitors at Hutzler's? Yes, but we want no Hutzlerites to Star!" The company also described its S*T*O*P SHORTAGES slogan as "Shortages Take Our Profits."[62]

Hutzler's appeared stable to everyday Baltimoreans and remained a very active corporate citizen, supporting important local institutions such as the Baltimore Museum of Art and Johns Hopkins University. The Towson store was still the leader of department store sales in the Baltimore metropolitan area and continued to be a fashion destination that appealed to a wide audience. Hutzler's Occasion Extraordinaire and Anniversary Sales still drew crowds. For many Baltimoreans, shopping trips to Hutzler's, especially to the Downtown or Towson stores, were family traditions. Hutzler's Downtown store was in an aging building in an aging business district, but it was nonetheless the mother store of the company. By 1972, the Downtown store fell to number three in sales behind Towson and Westview, but the Hutzler family was far from giving up its Downtown store.[63]

In the 1950s, Hutzler's carried a Pin Money Dress Department in its Downtown upstairs store. These housedresses were geared toward the 1950s housewife, and its name came from the idea that a woman had to pin money onto her dress due to the absence of pockets. By the 1970s, the store had phased out that department. Hutzler's also carried the popular Queen Casuals sportswear line. Queen Casuals consisted of 100 percent polyester pantsuits and coordinates that featured pants with elastic waistbands and no pockets. The clothing came in colors that were called "orange sherbet" or "mint green." Order forms were included in the monthly credit statements. The clothing was mainstream and was geared toward the stereotypic "Baltimore Hon."[64] "Queen Casuals was a line that you just wouldn't not carry," says buyer Sue Gaston Sachs. The line was not popular at the Towson location but had a loyal following at the Eastpoint and Southdale stores.

Hutzler's was a family business and had typical family problems, which led to open bickering about business decisions and practices. Some family members were angry that the store was not innovative. The merchandise offerings might have been original, but the company was not pioneering in trying to compete in price and selection with discounters like E.J. Korvette. Other members of the family strongly felt that "this business has worked for fifty years and we are not going to change it now." The store made small profits and tensions ran high. The Downtown store was a huge piece of property, and some family members questioned the expense in continuing to operate it. Family members also were beginning to question the future of the full-scale department store. "What I went through was the typical family business that was in a failing industry," says Albert D. Hutzler III.

In 1974 the company announced the opening of its sixth store. It was located in Salisbury, Maryland, and it was the first new location in almost a decade. However, the store only occupied fifty thousand square feet. Originally, the name of the store was to be Hutzler's Quality Fashions, as the store only carried ready-to-wear clothing for men, women and children. The store was built in a new wing of the Salisbury Mall, a "nothing mall" that also housed a Hecht Co. store as well as a Sears store.[65] Employees and family members questioned the motives to open its first new store in years in remote Salisbury. "Hutzler's was dormant for so long and the opening of the Salisbury store was a missed play," states former executive John Godfrey. Richard Hutzler recalls the Salisbury store as a "strange adventure. It was so far away and small."

Hutzler's first store in over a decade was opened in 1975 at the Salisbury Mall in Salisbury, Maryland. *Courtesy of the Baltimore County Public Library Legacy Web.*

George Hutzler Bernstein felt that Hutzler's began to lose its prestige by the late 1950s, and the opening of the Salisbury store reinforced this opinion. "We were trying to maintain a prestige image but we weren't putting stores in places that had prestige customers." Over the next few years, the Salisbury store made either slim profits or slim losses. It didn't contribute much to the company's bottom line. But the store did intensify the problems within the family. Albert D. Hutzler III feels that "unfortunately there were many disagreements among the family, to put it in nice terms." He continues, "With the demise of the store came the demise of the family."

To its customers, and especially to its employees, Hutzler's was still one big family. "I don't think that this family loved each other completely but you would not know that working there," says Dan Sachs, former merchandise manager. Employees felt a certain pride about having a job with Hutzler's. They were not overpaid but they were extremely loyal to their company. It wasn't unusual to have employees celebrate their twentieth, thirtieth or fortieth year with the store. Even former vice-president and treasurer George Hutzler Bernstein felt that "you were willing to work for less at Hutzler's" and was dismayed at how raises were arbitrarily distributed to its employees, sometimes taking advantage of their loyalties.

The company ended up handing the control of the stores to Charles G. Hutzler III. Charles was the great-grandson of store founder Charles G. Hutzler and had spent time learning the trade at L.S. Ayres & Co. in

Indianapolis before coming back to Baltimore. In 1962, he became assistant general merchandise manager and in the following year he became vice-president. He had also been active with community organizations such as the Baltimore Symphony Orchestra, the Sinai Hospital and the Maryland Children's Aid Society. Charles was well liked by the community, by the Hutzler employees and even by members of the Hutzler family. He was dedicated to the business and was a strong merchandiser. Getting Hutzler's house back in order was now Charles's job, and it was a tall order.

By 1976, Hutzler's was trying its hardest to stay afloat. Even the public began to notice the store's financial troubles. Hutzler's traditions, such as the annual calendar and the Howard Street Christmas windows, were dropped. After fifty-five years, the employee magazine, *Tips and Taps*, printed its final issue.

Hutzler employees were never part of the Retail Store Employees Union. However, since 1973, Local 692 had been trying to organize the workers of the Southdale store. In July 1976, union organizers began to hear word that Hutzler's was about to lay off a substantial number of its employees. The company responded that the store was reporting a decline in earnings and it needed to address what it saw as "excessive costs." Union officials felt that this was just an attempt to stymie the union's effort to organize. In the end, the vote to join Local 692 failed at Southdale, and only twenty of the store's three hundred employees lost their jobs.[66]

Many former employees interviewed felt that there was no need for organized labor unions at the stores. They were satisfied there and they felt appreciated for their work. The store was happy that it wasn't forced to work under the confines of a collective bargaining agreement.

When David A. Hutzler joined the board in 1976, he felt that "things were really rotten in Denmark." He also felt that there was great pressure for the company to change. Hutzler's president, Charles, decided that the answer to Hutzler's problems was to once again seek a merger with another firm. However, Charles decided to look closer to Baltimore, and more specifically, he decided to look across the street. Charles contacted the executives at the Hecht Co., thinking that the rival would be interested in buying Hutzler's out. Hecht's responded with a request to see many of Hutzler's financial documents before it would consider such a proposal. Realizing the sensitivity of such a demand, Charles tried to convince some of the Hutzler family members to permit him to give up some of this information. Board member David A. Hutzler recalls, "Charles lightly mentioned this upcoming meeting with officials with the Hecht Co. and his need to present sales information to them for them to review. I couldn't believe it. I said, 'You want to give the sales numbers from each department to the Hecht Co.?'"

Once the news surfaced that Charles had met with the Hecht Co. and given them some of Hutzler's financial information, a furor broke out in the boardroom. Lawyers argued, board members argued. Family members felt that Hecht's was negotiating deceptively, and everybody knew that the Federal Trade Commission would never allow such a merger. Soon the whole merger issue simply died away, but the family was more broken than ever before.[67] David A. Hutzler says, "I do think that Charles ended up taking some of the sales numbers over to the Hecht Co. And I'm sure the Hecht Co. was just delighted to see them."

Running a department store business on Howard Street proved to be an ongoing challenge. Reports showed that downtown Baltimore department stores sales fell from $93 million in 1972 to just $68 million in 1975. In its peak year of 1968, Hutzler's was reporting $22 million in sales from its Howard Street store. In 1977, that figure dropped to about $11.5 million. The Hecht Co. had sales of $19 million and saw its numbers drop to about $14 million. Even though its sales numbers dropped, Hecht's downtown store pulled in more sales than Hutzler's. Stewart's, always trailing in the back, had its downtown sales drop from $9 million in 1968 to $6 million in 1977.[68] But the news of the year 1977 came from Hochschild Kohn.

As far back as 1974, the City of Baltimore had compiled data on the downtown area and what effects new mass transit plans had on the area's revitalization. It was forecast in 1974 that "at least one and probably two of the major department stores in the retail area would close."[69] Consistent with that prediction, Hochschild Kohn announced in January 1977 that it would close its main downtown store.

Over the years, Hochschild's management had refused to put money back into the store. The company had stopped installing its famous Christmas windows back in 1965.[70] The store lost direction, and programs like "Leisure Suit Tuesdays" did nothing to help the store's image. Hochschild's officials acknowledged that the closing "had been in the mill for a long time" and offset the news of the downtown store's closing with reports that it would open three smaller locations in Baltimore's northern suburbs. Hochschild's called its downtown store, which dated from 1897 and was spread throughout eight buildings, obsolete. It complained that the store found it difficult to display merchandise with so many balconies and different levels. Hochschild's said that sales at its downtown location had dropped from 8 to 10 percent a year for the past four years.[71]

Shoppers at Howard and Lexington Streets on Hochschild Kohn's final day of operation on September 5, 1977. *Courtesy of Jacques Kelly.*

Charles Hutzler's told the media that he was not surprised at Hochschild's decision. "I hate to see a neighbor leave but we at Hutzler's have just spent time and money remodeling our store and it is our intention to stay." Charles also stressed that the Christmas 1976 season ended "fairly strongly" at all of his firm's stores. Officials at the Hecht Co. expressed their sadness at losing its neighbor. Stewart's refused comment.[72]

Every Friday morning, Hutzler's department heads met. One Friday morning in June 1977 would forever change the makeup of Hutzler's. Bob Eney, former visual merchandising manager, remembers it very well.

Charles came into the meeting room and said, "It's too damn hot in here." So, we called the engine room to check on lowering the temperature. The engine room called back and told us that the air was cranked up and we couldn't go any higher. Charles went back to his office and sat there for about five minutes. Charles was due in court at 1:00 p.m. that day as that was the day he was getting his divorce from Eleanor. He said it was still too hot. Charles began pacing the corridor outside of the conference room. Several times he passed by the door and finally he didn't. The executive secretary called out, "Charles is on the floor down here!" We ran down the corridor and Charles was struggling to breathe. They took him away in an ambulance and he died before he reached the hospital. It was awful. Everybody loved Charles Hutzler.

Richard Hutzler felt that Chuck was a "neat guy." He wonders, "Who knows what would have happened if Chuck lived?"

With Charles's death, Hutzler's lost its leader and one of the strongest fashion merchandisers that it ever had.[73] The store was a ship without a captain. Immediately following his death, the company's board of directors released a statement saying that "Charles' dedication to the company was in the finest family tradition." Hutzler's was forced to look outside its family for new leadership—a move that would help the company in some ways but would ultimately harm the relationship between the company and its loyal employees.

UNDER NEW MANAGEMENT

After Charles Hutzler's death, Albert Hutzler Jr. came back into power, but only temporarily. The family searched for Charles's replacement but couldn't find anyone who was interested in steering the ship, which was running off course. Carriage trade retailers had fallen out of fashion all across the country. And at Hutzler's, many employees felt that the handwriting was on the wall—the company was in unstoppable trouble by 1977.

Austin Kenly had joined the company before Charles's death in the position of chief financial officer. He came to Hutzler's from Black & Decker, where he had served as that company's assistant treasurer. In the absence of any other interested party, Kenly assumed the leadership of the company. However, Kenly's strength was in finance, and he had no experience in running or leading a family retail business. Former executive Dan Sachs says, "Austin Kenly was not brought in to be a merchandiser. He was brought in to straighten out the store, which he somewhat did."

Almost from day one, Kenly made changes that conflicted with the family image that Hutzler's had cultivated over the years with its employees. "Traditionally, executives would play card games during their free time in the break rooms, not in view of the customer. There was no betting involved, just simple card games. Within the first week, Kenly forbid employees from playing future card games," said Sachs. Kenly looked everywhere to cut costs. More importantly, he brought in outside management help. It was a move that proved unpopular with most of the Hutzler workers.[74]

Hutzler's tried to maintain its image as a fashion leader in Baltimore, but it was losing sales to the Hecht Co. Hecht stores appealed more to the general public, and with the backing of the May Department Stores Company, it was becoming a true powerhouse. Kenly was charged with running a fashion business but many Hutzlerites felt he didn't understand fashion. Kenly insisted that the company economize wherever possible. One of Kenly's first victims was Occasion Extraordinaire. Hutzler's had a history of sending buyers to Europe and the Far East to find unusual items and purchases that would set the company apart from the competition. Kenly nixed those plans and made the buyers look locally for cheaper merchandise for this special event.[75] "How do you economize and find something chic?" asks Bob Eney.

Kenly hired people from outside the company and area, and many of his choices were unpopular. Family board member David A. Hutzler states, "Austin brought in bright, energetic directors and then micromanaged them." The directors had strong résumés from other leading retailers but most had other plans for the traditional Hutzler image. "I don't understand why it is…when people come in from out of town, they don't try to learn the town…Just because they were successful somewhere else, they think that it's going to work in Maryland," says former employee Lynn Stecher Cox.

There were "strange faces" throughout the store and the Hutzler family faces were seen less and less. Lynn Stecher Cox remembers one Christmas plan shortly after Austin Kenly came into power:

> We all showed up at a meeting and were told that we were doing a "pink and blue Christmas." I couldn't believe it. I said that "I'm sorry but Maryland is a very traditional state. If you don't do green and red it's never going to fly." Well, they bought boxes, bags and trim and we put it all up. It was up for maybe a week or two and we got so many calls from people who hated the pink and blue colors. So we had to take it down and put up every decoration from past years and find every old Christmas box that we could. That pink and blue color scheme had to have cost the company thousands and thousands of dollars.

This wasn't the only image stumble that the company made.

In September 1977, the city announced a new plan for Howard and Lexington Streets called Baltimore Gardens. This project called for redevelopment of the block containing the recently closed Hochschild's store and Hutzler's South Building, or what was commonly referred to as the "Palace Building." The city announced that the buildings would be condemned and Hutzler's would receive fair market value for the 1888 structure. Though Hutzler's declined comment, it was revealed that the store had known about this plan for quite some time and the company was eager to raise any form of capital from wherever it could. Unfortunately, or fortunately, the plan never came to fruition, and the historic structure, which still housed offices and a newly remodeled Men's Department, remained.[76]

In October 1977, Hutzler's announced plans for its newest branch: a store located in the Inner Harbor section of downtown. It would contain only thirty-five thousand square feet of space on two levels and it had an anticipated opening of 1980. The company insisted that it was not meant to replace or compete with the Howard Street store. The branch would carry only ready-to-wear and luggage and it was hoped that it would capture some of the success of the newly developed harbor front area.[77]

Few longtime employees could make sense of this move. Like the Salisbury store, it didn't seem to fit the profile that the upper-end, all-purpose store was trying to present. Austin Kenly pushed the plans for the Inner Harbor store forward. "It wasn't even close to the Inner Harbor. We all thought they were crazy," says Dan Sachs. Even before the Inner Harbor store opened its doors, more controversy erupted in the company.

Barbara Bailey was one of the new faces at Hutzler's. Coming from I. Magnin & Co. in San Francisco, Bailey joined the company as the executive vice-president in charge of sales promotion. Her job was to update Hutzler's image and to promote the store specifically as a fashion store. Her tasks included modernizing the logo, updating its newspaper advertisements and painting and renovating some of the stores. The employees secretly balked when the new color scheme of the store became brown, also referred to on the inside as "Barbara Bailey brown."[78]

By now Hutzler's was in a slide, both in sales and employee morale. Once bustling and cheerful, employee events such as Christmas parties became "strange gatherings where we all just sat around like lumps."

The year 1979 was a noteworthy one. On January 2, 1979, Stewart's announced that it was closing its downtown store, across the street from Hutzler's Howard Street store. The store reported that it had been losing money downtown for the past four to five years. The closing was clearly a blow to the Howard Street retail area. Though it was known for quality merchandise, Stewart's had never commanded the full respect of the Baltimore consumer. "There were no Jewish people in the management of Stewart's, but that doesn't mean it wasn't a good store," says Bob Eney. He always respected Stewart's. "That's where the well-heeled lady would buy something for the kids and her husband but she still went to New York to buy her clothing." Now with Stewart's gone, there was one less reason for Baltimoreans to come downtown and shop.

Rumors began to swirl that Hutzler's might consider closing its Howard Street store. Kenly responded, "There does in fact come a point of no return. We haven't yet reached that point." In reaction to the gossip, the company spent over $2 million on renovations to its Downtown store as well as Eastpoint, Westview and Towson. Most of the money spent at the Downtown store was directed to the reduction of the selling area's size. Its 325,000 feet of sales space soon dropped down to just over 90,000 square feet.[79]

The year 1979 was also when "Black Friday" occurred. On Black Friday, all executives were called into the store. In a desperate attempt to cut costs and gain control over its employees, longtime executives were purged. Not all were dismissed, but enough were let go that almost all employee loyalty was shattered.[80] After the dust settled, it led to a showdown between Austin Kenly and the only remaining family member still active in the store's management, George Hutzler Bernstein. The boardroom battle resulted in hard feelings all around, and over the next few years tensions would continue to escalate.

In March 1980, the long-awaited Hutzler's Inner Harbor location opened. The *Baltimore News American* reported, "It's not going to be a place to buy a washing machine. The Hutzler's folks have fitted it out in shades of a maroony brown (or maybe it's a browny maroon)." Store officials promoted its "updated and contemporary look." It was clear that the store was geared to the working businessman and businesswoman in nearby buildings. But in the long run, it earned only a small following, and its meager earnings did not contribute to the store's overall meager profit base.

Hutzler's Towson store was still a fashion and merchandise leader. With sales of $25 million, it was the largest volume department store in the Baltimore metropolitan area. Because of the store's traditions and loyal customers, rival Bamberger's deemed the Towson store "our greatest competition from what we've seen so far in Baltimore."[81] That Christmas, the Towson store introduced the talking reindeer, Tinsel and Beau, and a new Baltimore tradition was born. Tinsel and Beau were later added to the Southdale and Westview locations.

In 1980, Hutzler's earned $65 million in sales, although that figure was down from $72 million in sales in 1972. The store was a large employer,

Hutzler's small two-level Inner Harbor store opened for business in March 1980. *Courtesy of Jacques Kelly.*

with 2,029 workers throughout the Baltimore area. The Howard Street store remained open, still home to elevator operators, real cream in its restaurants and a feeling that only a grand old department store could give. Though Hutzler's insisted that the downtown store "carried its own weight," it was expensive to operate and, as George Hutzler Bernstein put it, "way beyond its life."

Competing retail stores, such as Macy's (with its Newark, New Jersey–based Bamberger's division), Woodward & Lothrop and the rejuvenated Hecht Co. stores, put pressure on Hutzler's. "When Macy's came in, Kenly went crazy. He tightened the belt in all spending," says Bob Eney. Hutzler's had to go head to head with the new well-known stores from out of town. Its executives now realized that their only chance for survival lay in the suburbs, and the next opportunity for success was White Marsh.

In August 1981, Hutzler's opened its first full-scale suburban department store in sixteen years. The White Marsh Mall was developed by the Rouse Company and was located in a yet-to-be-named section of northeastern Baltimore County. The mall was just off Interstate 95 near the Baltimore

Beltway. Here was a chance for Hutzler's to boast a new prototype store and regain its image as a leading fashion store. More importantly, it was a chance for Hutzler's to show its muscle against newcomers Bamberger's (a division of parent company Macy's) and Woodward & Lothrop. Plus, it was an opportunity for Hutzler's to avoid competing with a Hecht's store.

It rained for days before the mall opened. The areas of dirt surrounding the new mall became pools of mud. As the store opened, a limo arrived with Hutzler's president Austin Kenly. George Hutzler Bernstein stated: "Here's a guy that shows up at the opening of the White Marsh store in a lime green polyester suit with white shoes. Now here's a guy that is supposed to be running a fashion business. He just didn't understand fashion." More devastating, the crowds did not arrive. Whether it was the rain or whether it was the customers' reluctance to try a new store, the White Marsh store had a dismal opening.

It became clear that Hutzler's had lost its place as Baltimore's premier image store. Many employees felt that the company was not going in the right direction. Prominent Hutzler workers gave notice. The empire began to crumble. The final showdown within store management between family and non-family members, which resulted in George Hutzler Bernstein's departure, was devastating. In February 1982, a consultant firm hired by Hutzler's advised the company to sell the business or face liquidation.

Opposite, top: A bird's-eye view of the main floor of the Downtown Hutzler's in 1980. *Courtesy of Jacques Kelly.*

Opposite, bottom: The White Marsh Mall Hutzler's was the last store that the company built from the ground up. It opened its doors in 1981. *Courtesy of the Jewish Museum of Maryland, 207.029.063.*

MAKING CHANGE

Hutzler's needed capital, and its expansive Towson parking lot was extremely valuable. As parcel after parcel was sold off for funds, the company finally agreed to lease a tract of the land to Hecht's. "We tried everything to keep the Hecht Co. out of Towson," says George Hutzler Bernstein. But money was money, and Hecht's had money and Hutzler's needed money. In September 1982, the Hecht Co. opened its new flagship location in Towson, practically adjacent to the Towson Hutzler's. It was named the flagship store for the Baltimore area, but its Howard Street store was not closed. Instead, Hecht's downsized its downtown store—every wall and floor was demolished in order to present a completely modern store. The downtown store was now modeled after its suburban stores. The renovation proved successful, and other May Company divisions traveled to Baltimore to see how a downtown store makeover could flourish.[82]

Baltimore's department store field narrowed when Associated Dry Goods announced that it was closing its entire Stewart's division by early 1983. Stewart's had been identified as a problem division for Associated Dry Goods for a number of years as it struggled to find its place in the Baltimore market. Though the store had been showing signs of improvement, its parent firm felt that the addition of Bamberger's and Woodward & Lothrop into the Baltimore retail scene was proving to be just too hard for Stewart's to compete. Associated Dry Goods announced that it would reopen its locations under the Caldor discount store banner.[83]

Hutzler's celebrated the opening of the Joseph Meyerhoff Symphony Hall with this souvenir shopping bag in 1982. *Courtesy of the Jewish Museum of Maryland, 1995.169.002.*

The 1980s were a time of massive change in the retail industry. Larger chains either gobbled up smaller department stores or closed their doors in massive numbers. It was necessary for retail stores to purchase inventory in large bulk in order to gain any discount benefits. Therefore, larger stores had an advantage over smaller stores—their buying strength scored lower prices from suppliers. In the 1980s, the whole face of retailing changed, but not for the good. "The extreme decline of the middle class eroded retailing and the whole department store industry in general," says Albert D. Hutzler III.

The biggest change to Baltimore retailing and Hutzler Brothers' history occurred in May 1983. The Hutzler family board decided that it was time to find a suitor, and along came Angelo Arena. Arena, with partner Edward Blair, purchased a controlling interest in the department store, making a large capital investment in Hutzler's, or what newspapers referred to as "an ailing giant." As part of the deal, family members retained their positions on the board of directors. Arena came to Hutzler's after serving as president and chief executive of Marshall Field & Co. in Chicago and Neiman Marcus of Dallas. He had a reputation as a progressive and controversial retailer.[84] "I didn't know much about Angelo Arena but I heard he was coming from Marshall Field and that sounded real good," remembers Richard Hutzler.

In an editorial titled "Hutzler's Fights Back," the *Baltimore Sun* praised the new leadership as "major league talent" and for bringing "an infusion of capital" to Hutzler's. The article continued:

> *Hutzler's—that great old name in retailing associated with Baltimore, with tradition, with quality and with one controlling family through six generations—has seemed to many shoppers to be in a holding pattern, trying to make its mind up what to do next. That, certainly, is the impression gained in the large, former flagship store."*

With Arena in charge, it was clear that things were going to change at Hutzler's.

Arena and Blair paid more than $7 million for their controlling interest in Hutzler's. With Arena at the helm, the company made some bold moves. Within three months, Arena announced that all operations, from retail to corporate, would move out of the famous Art Deco Downtown building into a new building to be constructed at the corner of Howard and Lexington Streets. Hutzler's would become part of the Atrium at Market Center being developed by the Murdock Development Company. It was on the site of the former vacant Hochschild Kohn store, which had been destroyed by a six-alarm fire on February 17, 1983. The store would shrink to just seventy thousand square feet over two and a half stories. Arena planned for a more upscale store with merchandise to match. The company worked out special subsidies with Baltimore city and then pledged to spend $4 to $5 million on the new store. The building would also incorporate the 1888 Palace Building into the new complex, and the store would officially be named Hutzler's Palace.[85]

In September 1983, Hutzler's announced further plans to open two to three stores in the next three to five years. The company considered expansion to less aggressive markets such as Wilmington, Delaware, Frederick, Maryland, and Newport News, Virginia. Proposals were also made to include the Towson store as part of a new Towsontown Centre, a 1.5-million-square-foot mall that, in addition to Hutzler's and Hecht's, would include anchors such as Saks Fifth Avenue and Garfinckel's. It would be the area's largest retail mall, and Hutzler's flagship Towson would be its main anchor store.

After the vacant Hochschild's store burned down, construction began from the ground up on the Murdock Co.'s Atrium at Market Center project. The project, seen here in 1984, included a brand-new downtown Hutzler's store. *Courtesy of Jacques Kelly.*

It was clear that Angelo Arena had big plans for his new retail empire and Baltimore's Hutzler department stores were only a part of it. "Angelo Arena and his crew came in and began to spend money like it was water," says former employee Lynn Stecher Cox. In January 1984, Arena purchased Boston-based Sara Fredericks, a ten-store chain of high-end women's shops that catered to the Palm Beach set.

In sharp contrast, the downtown Hutzler's store began phasing out many of its departments at its old Howard Street location. The famous downstairs luncheonette suddenly closed during that very same January. With its orange-stained wood chairs, its pink terrazzo floors and its neon sign, the luncheonette was a true Art Deco gem. Columnist Jacques Kelly stated,

> *The demise of the basement luncheonette was certainly the end of an era. The customers, probably even myself included, were characters. Even toward the end, when the customers were far fewer than before, they were no less cranky…Somehow, those grand waitresses always kept their temperatures normal and never grew irritated at the cranky demands of the people who lunched there.*

On August 21, 1984, Hutzler's acquired four stores from Hochschild Kohn. These stores were four of Hochschild's biggest and most profitable stores. Hochschild's had been in a retrenchment mode since closing its famous Belvedere store and had just announced the closing of its Reisterstown Road Plaza store. Its parent company, Supermarkets General, had pulled its interest out of Baltimore a number of years before. Supermarkets General closed the local Hochschild Kohn corporate office in 1983 and merged its operations with its Howland-Steinbach division based out of White Plains, New York. The transaction cost Hutzler's $10 million as the company grew to eleven stores. Finally, Hutzler's had the prize that it had been seeking for quite some time—Hochschild's store at the Security Square Mall.

Many analysts praised Arena's acquisition. One analyst, favoring the purchase, said, "Not too long ago, Hutzler's was on the brink. I'm glad to see them make a go of it."[86] Family members who remained on the board of directors were confident that Angelo Arena knew what he was doing. "We thought Arena was a genius, at first," says former board member David A. Hutzler.

In addition to acquiring the prime spot at Security Square, Hutzler's was ridding itself of one of its weaker competitors. The remaining four Hochschild's stores, small in size, limped along for another two years until they were converted into other use.

Hutzler's was hopeful that its sales would grow by 35 percent with the Hochschild purchase. This was easy to project since Hochschild's Security Square had historically been the Baltimore market's second highest grossing department store. Unfortunately, the new Security Square Hutzler's store

Hochschild's Security Square Mall store was Baltimore's second highest grossing department store. It became a Hutzler store in 1984. *Courtesy of the BGE collection at the Baltimore Museum of Industry.*

competed with the profitable Hutzler's Westview store just a couple of miles away. Furthermore, the Hochschild purchase actually resulted in two store properties within a short walk of each other at Eastpoint Mall.[87]

Due to his past leadership at Neiman Marcus and Marshall Field's, Angelo Arena seemed to have the support of the lending community. Not all Hutzler's employees were convinced about Arena's abilities or his motives. Former executive Nancy Thorn states, "I was always told that Angelo Arena bought Hutzler's as a tax write-off and I always believed that. Once I was in a meeting and the buyers were told, 'You don't let the customer tell you what they're going to buy, you tell the customer what they're going to buy.' That does not work in retail."

People began to wonder where Angelo Arena was getting his money. The company never had sufficient capital to cover its desire for growth. George Hutzler Bernstein states that Hutzler's had weathered its storms in the past because "the banks were really kind to us." Company insiders knew that the business was being stretched thin. Buyer Sue Sachs recalls

On the left, the new downtown Palace store nears completion in November 1984. *Courtesy of Jacques Kelly.*

Hutzler's began its moving sale in early January 1985, as it would soon depart its landmark Howard Street store for its new upscale Palace location. *Private collection.*

When you went into the New York market in the past, the vendors couldn't do enough for you. You would walk into a showroom and they would just go crazy for you. But during this time it wasn't public but they knew we were having credit problems. Later, the opening to buy was no longer there. You were trying to buy for eleven stores and there was no money to buy for eleven stores.

Being a buyer for Hutzler's was once an exciting job for a person in retailing. Now, with little cash left to stock the fleet of eleven stores, "we really stepped down the quality, and, as a buyer, it no longer was fun anymore. Now you had to find people who would sell to you," says Sachs.

In May 1984, the City of Baltimore purchased the old Howard Street Hutzler's store for $5.2 million. Renovations were completed by 1986, and the building was leased to the state for its Department of Human Resources to use as office space.

After the Christmas 1984 season, Hutzler's began to advertise its "Moving Sale" with a goal of opening the new Hutzler's Palace store at the fabled intersection of Howard and Lexington Streets by April 1, 1985. Angelo Arena's prized possession, his initial project dating back to his arrival in Baltimore, was almost complete. Arena put all his eggs into this basket, and the new store's success was crucial to the success and image of the company and its future.

EVERYTHING MUST GO

The day the Palace store opened it was a flop, a complete flop.
It was an utter failure.
—David A. Hutzler, board member, 1976–90

On April 1, 1985, Hutzler's unveiled its Palace store. The store opened with much fanfare and, according to Angelo Arena, marked the rebirth of Howard and Lexington Streets as a premier destination for retail shopping. The new store occupied less square footage than the former Howard Street location, but Arena pulled out all the stops and found ways to fill the store with mostly upscale merchandise.

The Palace store featured high-end clothing, including some designer fashions, along with decorative home furnishings. It also had a Gucci accessory collection and a "skylight bar and restaurant." Hutzler's was betting that the Palace store would bring well-heeled shoppers back to the area. Columnist Jacques Kelly was a supporter of the new Palace store. "I felt that Hutzler's probably had to change something." Unfortunately, the new store and its high-end merchandise with its high-end prices proved to be too much change for the new Howard and Lexington Streets intersection. It was a recipe for disaster.

When the Palace opened its doors, shoppers found beautiful clothing at "ridiculous" prices. Howard and Lexington Streets appealed to lower middle-income, inner-city shoppers.[88] The upscale customer never appeared. Howard Street had been under construction for years with the advent of Light Rail service. The street was a mudhole and a mess.

Left: Hutzler's 1985 Palace store at the intersection of Howard and Lexington Streets. *Photograph by the author.*

Below: Hutzler's celebrated Christmas 1985 with its "Bawlmer Bear" promotion. *Courtesy of Jacques Kelly.*

Arena had been assuring family board members that the mayor was fully behind the new store. However, as the building neared completion, Arena remarked that the new store might "be a tough sell" to the Howard Street market. This concerned company executives. The Hutzler's executives were also concerned that the Hecht Co. was being paid to rent out the upper floors of Hecht's downtown store.[89]

It was obvious that the Palace store's lack of business was going to seriously impact the company's finances. Arena knew that the "glitzy" store lost money in significant amounts from the day it opened. But that did not stop him from continuing to build his new retail empire.

In August 1985, Hutzler's announced that it would open a new store in Westminster, Maryland. The store would be smaller, similar to the company's Salisbury store. It would be a test store to see if Hutzler's could successfully open smaller stores in smaller markets. It would open in the spring of 1987.[90] Unfortunately, the Westminster Hutzler's was never built. Hutzler's had also pinned its hopes on a new suburban store at the Owings Mills Mall. Expected to be a powerhouse retail center for the Baltimore area, Owings Mills only agreed to allow Hutzler's to enter its second phase of construction. "We couldn't go ahead with a store in Owings Mills because we just didn't have the money. In those days, it would have cost $10 million to build a store," says George Hutzler Bernstein.

Shortly after the Westminster store was announced, Arena made public another large retail target. Arena acquired financial backing and support to purchase New York's B. Altman & Co. department store chain. B. Altman, a seven-store chain, was an institution in the Big Apple. It was a baffling move for many people involved in the retailing industry. "With Hutzler's in financial trouble, Arena's attempted purchase of B. Altman was similar to rearranging the chairs on the *Titanic*," says Albert D. Hutzler III. The project took precious time and effort from the day-to-day operations of the Hutzler's stores. Hutzler's was still trying to digest the new Hochschild's stores and was desperate to figure out what to do with the new Palace store. By January 1986, Arena's bid for B. Altman fell through and his attempt to enter the New York market failed.[91] Arena thought that he could compete in the retail market by continuing to grow Hutzler's. Unfortunately, the Hutzler community was most profoundly affected by Arena's failed dreams of growth. "Angelo Arena tried to make Hutzler's the Marshall Field's of the East. But it was like trying to raise a corpse," says former executive John Godfrey.

With Arena running around trying to expand the business, Richard Hutzler couldn't help but ask, "Who's watching the store?"[92] The year 1986 proved

We can serve you in so many ways:

- alterations
- bake shop
- bridal gift registry
- catering and party tray
- cleaning services:
  dry cleaning, drapery and rug cleaning, fur cleaning and storage, glove cleaning, in-home cleaning, suede and leather cleaning
- credit plans:
  option account, extended payment account and tabletop club
- deluxe gift wrap
- engraving and printing
- gift certificates
- gift hotline
- hairworks salon
- handicapped customer service
- Literary Guild book club
- Loyola Federal
- magazine subscriptions
- phone order service
- portrait studio
- repairs:
  handbags, jewelry and watches, razors, ring mounting, silverplating, weaving
- restaurants
- shoe bronzing
- shop-at-home decorating service
- silk flower arranging
- two-week return policy

  • Palace • Towson • Westview
  • Eastpoint • Salisbury • Inner Harbor
  • White Marsh • Harundale
  • Harford • Security Square

A directory listing all of Hutzler's services when the store was at its peak of ten locations. *Author's private collection.*

to be a tough one for the company. It was clear that the Palace store's lack of sales jeopardized the entire company. Many members of the Hutzler family wondered if their company was ever going to recover from these mistakes. "By 1986, it was all out of the family's hands. It was a fiasco. The company was off in six different directions with no plan. By then it was far too gone to salvage," states George Hutzler Bernstein.

By the end of 1986, the Downtown store was losing money quickly and draining profits from the other stores in the company. Hutzler's tried to reduce the rent at its Palace location and explored the possibility of breaking the lease. The lease agreement between Hutzler's and the Murdock Co. was firm. David Murdock reminded Arena that he held a fifteen-year lease at the Palace location and the lease could not be broken unless the store filed for bankruptcy.[93] Realizing that the company couldn't continue to support two downtown locations, Hutzler's decided to close its Inner Harbor store in December 1986. More store closures were just right around the corner.

The company continued a downward spiral through 1987. The store constantly tried to get out of its Palace store lease. "The company was being put on 'Cash Before Delivery' status. Department stores can't operate that way," says David A. Hutzler. In March, Hutzler's announced that it would close its locations in the Salisbury Mall, the Harford Mall (a former

Thomas Taylor vacuums the floor of the recently closed Westview store on October 13, 1987. *Courtesy of the Baltimore County Public Library Legacy Web.*

Hochschild Kohn store) and the Westview Mall, a signature long-running store for the company. These drastic moves turned the company into a six-store chain, down from its peak of eleven. Hutzler's problems were far from over and its stores, along with the store's image, began to suffer greatly.

By 1987, many people felt that Hutzler's was too far gone to salvage. Former family members and employees were heartbroken that the Hutzler name was still attached to the stores. It was hard for people like former buyer Sue Gaston Sachs just to walk into the stores. Sachs says, "After all of the years that I worked there, I couldn't go back into the stores after I left. It was so depressing to see the dive that it was taking. I think I went in once or twice during that first year and then I never went in again."

Angelo Arena was frantic for money, and in April 1987, he sold a 50 percent share of Hutzler's to Ohio businessman Jerome Schottenstein.[94] Schottenstein, owner of the Value City discount chain, was known for purchasing troubled companies and eventually liquidating them. It was a desperate move. "Schottenstein sucks the life out of companies that are on their knees," says David A. Hutzler.

Schottenstein brought merchandise back into the stores and also helped the company out of some of its more difficult leases. But the merchandise was not representative of Hutzler's former prestige image, and shoppers still stayed away.

In June 1987, Hutzler's said that it would close its Palace store if there was not a significant rent reduction from the Murdock Co. Arena threatened to close the store by July and blamed the store's problems on the promises that were unfulfilled by the Murdock Co. Murdock had planned to build large office towers in the Lexington Market area, promising hordes of potential shoppers through the large mass of offices. Those buildings were never built. Arena decided to show that he was serious with his request for a rent reduction and began holding an "across the board" sale at the Howard Street store. The intersection of Howard and Lexington Streets was in shambles.

People began to panic over the future of Howard and Lexington Streets. The Hutzler's store was failing and the Hecht Co. store was making rumblings about its future. "At the end, it was only the two stores, Hutzler's and Hecht's, left, and you know the writing was on the wall for the Hecht Co. too," observes Jacques Kelly. The leaders of Lexington Market called for a meeting with then Mayor William Donald Schaefer. "I remember sitting in William Donald Schaefer's office with the board of directors of Lexington Market. We were talking about what should be done with Howard and Lexington Street and how it should be revived. Schaefer loudly stated, 'It will never be the same so forget about it!' You could build the Taj Mahal at Howard and Lexington but the people wouldn't come back," says Bill Devine, co-owner of John W. Faidley Seafood in Lexington Market.

With the lease battle still up in the air, Hutzler's temporarily closed its Palace store. In the meantime, in order to stay alive, Hutzler's focused its energy on some of its remaining suburban stores. The company started with its Towson location. The *Baltimore Sun* reported "The work going on at Hutzler's Towson store is richly symbolic of the final stage in a critical metamorphosis aimed at keeping Baltimore's oldest department store chain alive." Arena moved 250 corporate executives housed in the 1888 Palace Building to new quarters on the upper floor of the Towson store. The Security Square location also received significant renovations. With the Christmas season right around the corner, the fate of Hutzler's would be decided within months.

Hutzler's was never a big moneymaker, even during its glory days. Now the store was in a fight for survival. Arena sold the Sara Fredericks stores in order to raise money, later claiming that he made a large profit on the deal. But he still had to find additional capital, so he sold the Towson store to a West Coast developer in a $15.2 million sale-leaseback transaction. The sale of the Towson store allowed Arena to buy out Jerome Schottenstein's 50 percent interest, and Hutzler's was finally back under his control. The Palace store reopened, but the location was sparsely stocked with lower-end merchandise. It was not a permanent solution for the ailing location.

"I personally felt that they tried real hard on Howard Street and all of the downtown redevelopment forces turned against them," states columnist Jacques Kelly.

Maybe the clearest sign that Hutzler's was in trouble came from the Towson store's Valley View Room restaurant. "When the Jell-O got the axe at Hutzler's Towson, it was the beginning of the end," stated a *Towson Times* article. Since its beginning, the Valley View Room had always served its chicken pot pie with fruit Jell-O. Budget cuts forced that to change. In its heyday, the restaurant "sucked in every unemployed woman in the Dulaney Valley for lunch or tea after tennis or shopping." The restaurant had a fiercely loyal yet typically older clientele. For sixteen years, Anne Benson ran the Valley View Room. In 1981, new management came to the store and requested that she cut costs. Along with the fruit Jell-O, the crab imperial and the store's famous pie pastry crust were all eliminated. The crust was substituted with a cheaper puff pastry that was difficult for the older customers to chew. When Benson was forced to change the famous blue cheese salad dressing recipe, she reached her breaking point. She was told to use cottage cheese in the blue cheese dressing and people wouldn't know the difference. "Oh God, that upset me," recalled Benson. "I guess I was just getting older and dottier by then and I just wanted to get the hell out of there." Soon she did leave, and all the personal touches that made the Valley View Room a destination left with her. The *Towson Times* reported in 1988, "Like the restaurant, the store itself is not what it used to be. Clucking and tsk-tsking, people whisper about its possible demise as they would about a wealthy woman who had succumbed to drink."[95]

On September 6, 1988, Hutzler's announced that it was going to close the Downtown store, this time for good. Arena had failed to get concessions out of David Murdock. The city still was owed a $2 million urban development loan that was set up to help finance the opening of the new Palace store back in 1985. The city was willing to forgive $850,000 of the debt but it was not enough for Arena to keep the store. Though many Baltimoreans mourned the upcoming loss of the store, they hadn't set foot in the store for the last decade.[96]

Two weeks later, Arena made a last-ditch effort to retain the downtown store. The Palace, a fiasco from day one, was his idea, after all. Arena decided not to close the store but to turn it into a discount format.[97] He would also try the same discount format at the Harundale Mall store. Harundale Mall was built in 1958 in Glen Burnie, Maryland, and was one of the first shopping malls in the country. The Harundale Hutzler's location was formerly a

Elderly diners dine at the Towson store's Valley View Room in September 1988. *Courtesy of the Baltimore County Public Library Legacy Web.*

Hochschild's Harundale Mall store, shown here in 1958, became a Hutzler's store in 1984. In a desperate attempt for survival, Hutzler's turned the Harundale store into a discount store format in September 1988. It closed three months later. *Courtesy of the BGE collection at the Baltimore Museum of Industry.*

Hochschild Kohn store that had replaced the Southdale Hutzler's store back when Hutzler's was on its buying spree in 1984. The plan to go discount "came out of left field" and was one of the final times Angelo Arena openly discussed his crumbling empire. From this point on, the public read about Hutzler's future only through its newspaper advertisements announcing clearance sales.

Within a month, Howard and Lexington Streets received the next major dose of horrible news. The Hecht Co. announced that it would close its Howard Street store after the Christmas 1988 season. The company regretted having to close the downtown store but stated that profits over the past few years were unacceptable.[98]

The downtown Hecht Co. still rang up $13 million in sales, but it could not compete against the stores by the harbor. With the closure of the downtown Hecht's, the classic mold of the traditional department store of the 1950s was broken. Now all that was left was a discount Hutzler store.

Hutzler's went ahead and celebrated its annual October Occasion Extraordinaire with whatever merchandise it could. But in November 1988, the Baltimore community opened its newspapers and learned through an advertisement that the Harundale Mall store would close. A clearance

sale was also announced at the Downtown store. Arena did not send out an elaborate press release or hold any special employee meetings. The company was hard up for cash, and Harundale was the next target. The Rouse Co., Hutzler's landlord, also learned about the closing through the newspaper advertisement. Once again, Angelo Arena was missing.

The company entered 1989 battered and bruised with four stores, plus a discount operation at the downtown Palace site. Hutzler's final sale was held in that year. By the end of January, Loyola Federal announced that it was severing its relationship

"The Best of Friends at Christmas" was the slogan for the store's final holiday season in 1988. *Private collection.*

The last two department stores on Howard Street, Hutzler's and the Hecht Co., as they appeared in January 1989. *Photograph by the author.*

The downtown Hecht Co. store at its final clearance sale in January 1989. *Photograph by the author.*

with Hutzler's. Loyola operated small branch operations in the Hutzler stores, and with a dwindling customer base, the bank decided that the branches were no longer productive. Out of the public eye, Angelo Arena leaked a memo saying that the Palace store was going to close shortly.

On February 18, 1989, a downtown Baltimore era ended as the Palace store, once a ritzy outlet that carried designer merchandise, closed its doors for the last time as a downtrodden clearance center.[99] It was no surprise that the store closed. The retail hub of Howard and Lexington Streets had virtually disappeared. People had moved from the city core into Baltimore's northern and western suburbs.[100] Gone were the bustling stores and the shouts of street vendors.[101] The old Howard and Lexington Street retail scene was now closed for business, at least for the department stores.

For the first time since the Civil War, there was no longer a Hutzler business operating out of downtown Baltimore. Many people mourned the loss of the store. Many of those people stated that they had meant to visit the new Palace store but just never made it there. Some loyal customers like columnist Jacques Kelly remained loyal to the Downtown store until the bitter end. Kelly vividly remembers his last visit to the store. He states, "I went to the Downtown store when they were about to close. It was a cold, bleak, winter day. I had parked in the Lexington Market parking garage, which is a high-rise structure. I looked out over at Hutzler's and I was just overcome with sadness. It was the feeling that you get at a bad funeral."

The Security Square store was next. Once the prize of the 1984 Hochschild Kohn purchase, the store was posting losses. News leaked in April that it would close. The company found a way out of its lease and the closing helped Hutzler's keep its lights on a while longer.

Hutzler's was at the point of no return. All hope was lost. The remaining family members on the board couldn't believe what had happened to their company. Family board member David A. Hutzler remembers, "When the stores started to close, I kept myself away from it. I just didn't want to be there." Employee morale was nonexistent on the sales floor and also in the offices. A handful of buyers remained and only a fraction of the sales force was at work, as so many had been let go. A very limited number of manufacturers would even accept orders from the store.[102] With only three stores left, Hutzler's buying power was peanuts. All that was left would soon end.

At the end of August 1989, Angelo Arena learned that Westinghouse Credit would no longer advance him cash for the remaining three stores to stock their shelves for the Christmas season. He knew that it was over.[103]

Above: A nighttime view of the White Marsh Mall Hutzler's as it holds its liquidation sale in 1989. *Photograph by the author.*

Left: In October 1989, Hutzler's announced that it was closing its last store, its flagship in Towson. *Photograph by the author.*

The Towson Hutzler's store just days before its closure in January 1990. *Photograph by the author.*

Most of the executive staff was dismissed, and Schottenstein came back to wind down the business.[104] Slowly but surely, the last three stores fell. The Eastpoint store, with its thinning merchandise selection, announced its closing in late September. It was quickly followed by the White Marsh Mall store, Hutzler's last attempt to build a store from the ground up. With Eastpoint and White Marsh now in their last days, all that was left was the crown jewel flagship store in Towson.

With Arena nowhere to be seen, Hutzler's advertised total liquidation of its Towson store in the October 15, 1989 *Baltimore Sun*. It was the nail in the coffin, marking the end of a once proud retailing institution. Customers cited the "loss of tradition" and compared the closure to "kind of like losing the Baltimore Colts." The Towson store, the last of the lot, closed its doors in January 1990. It was all over.

It was one of the slowest declines in department store retailing. Customers had nothing left but memories of the Baltimore institution, and for most, it was better than watching an old friend die a slow death.

CLOSEOUT

It's too bad that the institution had to disappear from the scene so ignominiously.
It just died. It's hard to see a great lady like that just die.
—Gilbert Sandler, Baltimore historian

In the end, what happened to Hutzler's? What happened to downtown department stores in general? In 1979, Martin B. Kohn of Hochschild Kohn probably best answered these questions. After the downtown Hochschild's store closed in 1977 and Hochschild Kohn had opened numerous branch locations throughout Baltimore and beyond, Kohn stated,

> *Did we lead or follow the flight of middle-income families from the city?*
> *It left the inner city mostly low income, with great demands on city services*
> *and a shrunken tax base. Among the problems that followed were poor*
> *schools, increased crime and high taxes. Department store business had been*
> *built on service, plenty of sales help, liberal return and credit policies, big*
> *assortments, integrity, interesting promotion and prime locations.*

Good service had become too expensive, and stores were reducing their merchandise selection in order to address their decline in sales volume. "The smart ones are adapting, the weak ones are passing," said Kohn.[105]

Hutzler's did pass. Its merchandise and its service were unparalleled, yet customers watched their favorite department store spiral downward for almost a decade. The last few years were especially tragic, as Baltimore's arguably greatest department store gradually resembled a discount store.[106] In an article in the *Towson Times*, Paul Milton stated, "Hutzler's became the victim of its own dreams. Angelo Arena wanted to make Hutzler's the Neiman Marcus of Baltimore. Unfortunately for him, Baltimore didn't want a Neiman Marcus. It wanted Hutzler's." And by 1990, Baltimore had neither.

As the company was wrapping up its business, family board member David A. Hutzler was very glum about the whole situation. He remembered a mailman coming to the door to deliver a package. The mailman mentioned how he looked so unhappy and David told him how he just felt terrible about what had happened to the family business. The mailman responded, "Yeah, but you did pretty good for 135 years." David Hutzler felt that "the mailman put it together better than I did."

David Hutzler was one of four family members who remained on the board of directors until the bitter end. "I debated departing for liability reasons and I debated staying because the family needed representation and nobody else was willing to do it," he said, adding, "When things go sour, everyone starts suing each other." All in all, the Hutzler family was able to walk away from the situation with some decent return on its centuries-old retail investment. Angelo Arena closed the business up and the company never had to file a bankruptcy petition.

Albert D. "Jiggs" Hutzler III stated that being a Hutzler family member in Baltimore was a real "privilege." His family was devoted to the city, and he felt that Baltimoreans put his family on a pedestal. After the store closed, he found that within a couple of years people "didn't know how to spell his name."

Even though he was a Hutzler, David Hutzler was never a fashion dresser. At parties, people couldn't exactly remember his last name. People called him David Hochschild, David Stewart or David Hecht. After a while, he asked to simply go by the name "David Department Store."

George Hutzler Bernstein was the last family member to help manage the department store chain. As he left the company in 1982, he felt that Hutzler's "had tried to become something that it just couldn't be."

Baltimoreans have memories about the store beyond its demise. There were visits to its restaurants, its festivals, its fashion shows and its Christmas displays. Resident Esther Max remembered taking the streetcar downtown and going to Howard and Lexington Streets and Read's Drug Store. "We would either eat at Read's and go shopping or we ate at Hutzler's." Ruth Greenfield recalled the service and the merchandise. She appreciated how the merchandise was well organized and displayed. "It was easy to shop there," she said. She then added, "And the people were happy that you shopped there." Both women felt that Nordstrom has taken Hutzler's place in the Baltimore market. "Nordstrom's is like what Hutzler's used to be," said Greenfield.

Many employees foresaw Hutzler's fate even as early as the 1970s. The store's technology was lagging behind.[107] The grand old department stores were falling out of favor and social changes were not helping to ensure their futures. Hutzler's insiders knew that the store never made enough money and what money was made was not invested properly. The Downtown store outlived its usefulness by many years, and small outlets such as Salisbury and Inner Harbor were costly to operate and became a detriment to the company.[108] But during its glory days, employees were one close family and were very proud of the operation.

After the store closed in 1990, some employees would occasionally meet to catch up with the families that were left behind when the business folded. A group of employees from the Eastpoint store would meet at least once a year. In February 1995, a group of Hutzlerites met and jokingly talked about having a reunion of all past Hutzler employees. They didn't have any money for such an event but wondered "what if?" Soon, Dan Sachs, a former merchandise manager, and his wife Sue, a former buyer, found themselves heading up a full-fledged Hutzler's reunion. More than six months' of preparation included speaking with 1,500 past employees and finding a location to meet. After publicity in the *Baltimore Sun* and promotion from WJZ-TV, 635 former Hutzlerites gathered one last time on August 26, 1995, at the Holiday Inn Select in Timonium, Maryland. "The only problem with the affair is that we should have done it all day," says Sachs. But it was a lot of painstaking work. The *Towson Times* appropriately called the event "Occasion Extraordinaire." The reunion was "the crowning glory to the end" of the company and truly culminated the end of an era. Former buyer Sue Gaston Sachs beautifully remembers what it was like to see the entire Hutzler employee family once again. Sachs says,

Our reunion was so much a wrap-up of all that Hutzler's was for us (meaning all of us who loved being a part of it). People come and go, work for years, retire, move away, pass away, then the company goes out of business and the link is broken. By having the reunion, we truly were a family once again and it was indeed a wonderful almost magical event!

Above: People attend the Hutzler's employee reunion in August 1995. *Courtesy of Dan and Sue Sachs*.

Left: Tinsel and Beau, Hutzler's famous talking reindeer, make an appearance at the reunion in August 1995. *Courtesy of Dan and Sue Sachs*.

It is clear that the spirit of Hutzler's lives on, both with events such as the 1995 reunion and in the memories of former customers, employees and Marylanders. The Howard Street store remains noble, as its exterior is protected with "historical status" from any type of future modifications. Now the home to the State Department of Human Resources, the interior of Hutzler's has been thoroughly gutted. Its Art Deco gems and treasures were thrown out in 1986 as the state outlined strict guidelines for the appearance of each office in the old building.[109]

But perhaps the spirit of Hutzler's truly lives on. Stories circulate that the building is home to the strange distant ringing of bells late at night. During late-night tours of the structure, building security guards frequently hear the bells or the jingle of keys, especially on the sixth floor, home of Hutzler's former signature restaurants and its beauty salon. These bells can also be heard on the fifth, seventh and eighth floors. There is no explanation for them.[110] Perhaps the building is still truly being watched and taken care of.

So whether one has pleasant memories of trips downtown on a streetcar or vivid recollections of visiting one of the store's many suburban stores or believes that the Howard Street store is still the home of one or two phantom Hutzlerites, the spirit of Hutzler's continues today. The store rightfully has earned its motto: "A Maryland Institution Since 1858."

CUSTOMER SERVICE

Hutzler's was a family-owned business that was devoted to the customer and the city. It was one of the "Grand Old Things of Baltimore." At Hutzler's, the accent was on service and quality. Those two ingredients helped set it apart from the other large Baltimore stores.

Almost twenty years have passed since the final doors were locked in 1990. However, the mere mention of the name Hutzler brings back a flurry of fast and fond memories. These thoughts come from Hutzler family members, former employees, dignitaries and everyday citizens, proving that the store served its customer, and the city of Baltimore, very well.

"Hutzler's was like your mother; they took care of you."
—Ruth Greenfield, Baltimore

"It's sad to see that all of the old department stores had to leave us. I always liked Hutzler's. They had a wonderful bakery and the chocolate cake was fabulous. That's where we used to meet, on the balcony."
—Esther Max, Baltimore

"Hutzler's was a Baltimore institution. It was the place you went with your mom to buy what made an IND girl cool—from the plaid skirts with bobby socks you wore to flirt with the boys on the weekends, to the prom dress that made you feel like a princess."
—Senator Barbara Mikulski, (D) Maryland

"The Hutzler family was a class act. They were delightful people."
—Bill Devine, co-owner, John W. Faidley Seafood, Lexington Market

"I loved Hutzler's. It was a pleasure because it was our high-class store at the time. The other stores were nice but Hutzler's was the posh store. The shrimp salad from the Tea Room was excellent and it was served with its signature cheese bread. It was a place for special occasions."
—Nancy Faidley-Devine, co-owner, John W. Faidley Seafood,
Lexington Market

"It was a family-oriented store and we were all a part of that family."
—Lynn Stecher Cox, visual merchandising, 1958–82

"I loved the fashion shows out at Goucher College. We would go for a week and take over the auditorium. It cost a lot of money and it was packed with kids."
—Bob Eney, visual merchandising manager, 1976–80

"I went to Hutzler's for all of my back-to-school clothes. To me, Hutzler's was the class act. Hutzler's, Stewart's, Hochschild Kohn, Hecht's. I think that was kind of the pecking order when I was young. Whether that was correct I don't know because I went to all of them basically."
—John Waters, filmmaker

"If anybody wanted to go shopping, they went to Hutzler's first."
—Dan Sachs, divisional merchandise manager, 1958–81

"Old-time Baltimoreans were very proud of Hutzler's because it was a store that was better than it needed to be. It gave so much back. It gave so much value for its money. It was progressive without being irritating."
—Jacques Kelly, columnist, *Baltimore Sun*

"Hutzler's was always a family company. My earliest memories of Hutzler's are getting on the streetcar at Register Avenue and York Road with my mom and having an excursion downtown shopping. Hutzler's was the main destination, although we shopped sometimes in Stewart's as well."
—Sue Gaston Sachs, buyer, 1969–85

"Hutzler's was an organization with a conscience."

—Richard Hutzler, grandson of store founder David Hutzler

"Hutzler's was a traditional store that had high-end customers that liked high-end merchandise. Over the years they lost track of their customer. I was fortunate to work at Hutzler's. It was a wonderful experience. It was a wonderful store in its heyday."

—John Godfrey, divisional merchandise manager, 1976–84

"We were very proud of the store. People still respond to us and have very fond memories of it."

—Rosemary Hutzler, daughter of Richard Hutzler

"It was the Grande Dame of Baltimore. In its heyday, it was a very special place with a wonderful loyal staff."

—George Hutzler Bernstein, vice-president and treasurer, 1960–82

"It was a nice way to grow up. It was a life. It was a family. It was an institution that was involved in shaping the life of the city. The Hutzler family was very devoted to Baltimore."

—Albert D. "Jiggs" Hutzler III, vice-president, 1964–76

"My father would sometimes drop me off at Toytown. I was a coin collector and he told me that if I behaved myself I could go to the cash room and count coins. On special occasions I did and I was able to pull out the special quarters."

—David A. Hutzler, board member, 1976–90

"Hutzler's was a first-class place. I used to think it was the best store but then I got into a debate on that with Hochschild Kohn."

—Governor William Donald Schaefer, governor of Maryland, 1987–95, mayor of Baltimore, 1971–87

"I loved Hutzler's. It was a very classy store. It was one of the big Baltimore traditions. The store had such a hometown feel. I don't know what it was about Hutzler's. Maybe it was because it was so 'Baltimore-ish' and very classy."

—Sam Moxley, Baltimore County councilman

"I was a teenager when I went downtown. I remember Christmastime, it was so fun. At Christmastime, two or three of us would go to Howard Street and visit all of the department stores. We would go from store to store but we always started at Hutzler's because it was always the most festive. Their windows were beautiful. If we could afford it we would go to the Tea Room. It was such a happy time. It's something that you just can't do these days."

—Barbara Cromwell, program coordinator,
Preservation Society of Fell's Point

"The accent was on service and on uncompromising quality. When you put the two together you get the 'Hutzler élan.' Everything about it spoke class."
—Gilbert Sandler, Baltimore historian

"It was a great store to work for. They trusted you. They cared about their customers and they cared about their employees. It was a great place. I miss it every day."

—Nancy Thorn, executive, 1960–89

"There was nothing else like it. The merchandise, the service, the displays, the variety, the quality. When I was a girl I lived in Perry Hall. At Christmas time it was like going to a wonderland. For a kid from the sticks it was second best to going to New York. It was a magical experience. The Hutzler employees knew their inventory and they were there to serve you. Its closing was the end of an age."

—Ellen von Karajan, executive director,
Preservation Society of Fell's Point

"My grandmother took me to Hutzler's on Howard Street every other Saturday. I remember their great decorations at Christmastime. Every year I was so excited to see them and I always looked forward to it."

—Mayor Sheila Dixon

"I loved the Hutzler store and I loved to go to the Tea Room and the Quixie. I was so sorry when the store was finished. Everybody in the city regrets it now. Once I was in the gift shop of the Baltimore Museum of Art and the clerk asked me for my last name. When I told her it was Hutzler she burst into tears. She was a former employee and she told me that the happiest days of her life were at Hutzler's."

—Bernice "Bunny" Stein (Mrs. Albert D. Hutzler Jr.)

Hutzler's Howard Street store as it appeared for the Christmas season in 1974. *Courtesy of the Jewish Museum of Maryland, (above) 1995.169.102; (below) 1995.169.011.*

FROM THE HUTZLER KITCHENS...

CRAB CAKES

1 egg, beaten
3/4 teaspoon dry mustard
1/8 teaspoon cayenne pepper
1-1/2 Tablespoon Worcestershire sauce
1/4 teaspoon salt
1 Tablespoon chopped parsley
1-1/2 Tablespoon mayonnaise
2 slices of bread, chopped into crumbs
1 pound backfin crabmeat

Mix all ingredients together, except for the crabmeat. Slowly fold the crabmeat into the other ingredients, being careful not to break apart any lumps. Fry crab cakes for a few minutes on each side and place under broiler.

Imperial Crab

1/2 cup mayonnaise
1/2 teaspoon Worcestershire sauce
1/2 Tablespoon dry mustard
1 teaspoon salt
1/4 teaspoon pepper
2 Tablespoons chopped green and/or red pepper
1 pound backfin crabmeat

Mix together mayonnaise, Worcestershire sauce, mustard, salt, pepper and chopped pepper. Add crabmeat and be careful not to shred the crab. Spoon mixture into four shells and dot with butter. Bake for twenty minutes at 350 degrees.

Baked Crab and Shrimp Casserole

1 pound crabmeat
1 pound medium deveined shrimp
1 cup mayonnaise
1/2 cup chopped green pepper
1/4 cup chopped onion
2 cups chopped celery
1/2 teaspoon salt
1 Tablespoon Worcestershire sauce
2 cups crushed potato chips
paprika

Mix together all ingredients except for the potato chips and paprika. Place the mixture into a large casserole dish. Cover with potato chips and sprinkle with paprika. Bake uncovered at 400 degrees for fifteen minutes and place cover over dish for an additional ten minutes.

Deviled Filet of Cod

6 cod filets
salt, pepper
3/4 cup oil
1 Tablespoon prepared mustard
dash of cayenne pepper
dash of curry powder
1 Tablespoon vinegar
1 clove garlic
1/2 teaspoon paprika
1 teaspoon prepared horseradish
bread crumbs

Sprinkle fish filets with salt and pepper. Mix together oil, mustard, cayenne pepper, curry powder, vinegar, garlic, paprika and horseradish. Marinate the cod in the oil mixture for thirty minutes. Roll cod in bread crumbs and sprinkle fish with oil. Lay cod on lightly greased broiling pan and broil slowly until cooked.

Scampi di Marsala (from Festa Italiana)

2 pounds shrimp
1/2 cup flour
1/2 cup olive oil
1/2 cup dry Marsala wine
2 teaspoons tomato paste mixed with 3 Tablespoons warm water
1 scallion, chopped
salt and pepper to taste

Dredge shrimp in flour. Sauté shrimp in oil for 3 minutes. Drain shrimp and reserve the oil. Cook shrimp and wine for five minutes. Then add the reserved oil, tomato paste, scallions and salt and pepper. Simmer for five minutes. Stir in small amount of lemon juice and serve.

SPAGHETTI A LA CARUSO (FROM FESTA ITALIANA)

6 chopped onions
3/4 cup butter
2 large cans chopped tomatoes
3 cans gravy
3/4 cup oil
12 ounces chopped mushrooms
3 cups chicken livers
3 teaspoons salt
1-1/2 teaspoons pepper
3 teaspoons lemon rind
6 Tablespoons chopped parsley
3 pounds spaghetti

Cook onions in butter until soft. Add tomatoes and gravy and simmer for ten minutes. Heat oil and sauté mushrooms and chicken livers. Add mushrooms, chicken livers and all remaining ingredients (except spaghetti). Cover and simmer for fifteen minutes. Serve over cooked spaghetti.

HUTZLER'S SHRIMP SALAD

2-1/2 pounds medium shrimp, chopped into pieces
2-1/2 pounds large shrimp, chopped into pieces
1/2 teaspoon dry mustard
1-1/2 pound diced celery
1-1/2 teaspoon Old Bay seasoning
2-1/2 cups mayonnaise
salt and pepper

Squeeze shrimp well and set aside. Mix remaining ingredients together and then mix with shrimp. Refrigerate well.

HUTZLER'S CHEESE BREAD

1 cake or package yeast
1 cup lukewarm water
9-1/2 cups bread flour
2 teaspoons salt
1/4 cup sugar
1 pint milk
13-1/2 ounces grated sharp cheese
2-1/4 Tablespoons margarine
2-1/4 Tablespoons butter

Dissolve yeast in water. Knead all ingredients together while slowly adding flour. Cover and let mixture rise until it is double in size, about two hours. Divide dough into two equal parts and place into two greased 4x8 bread pans. Cover and let dough double in size. Bake for one hour at 300 degrees.

CHOCOLATE CHIFFON PIE

1/4 pound grated sweet chocolate
1 pint milk
1 ounce unflavored gelatin
8 eggs, separated
1/4 pound sugar
1/2 teaspoon salt
1 pound sugar
2 pie shells, baked

Melt chocolate in milk. Soften gelatin in cold water in ¼ cup cold water. Stir into chocolate mix. Add eight egg yolks beaten with ½ cup sugar. Add salt and cool.

Beat sugar into egg whites. Fold egg whites into chocolate mixture. Pour into two baked pie shells. Chill until firm and top with whipped cream.

WELLESLEY FUDGE CAKE

2 cups margarine
6 cups sugar
12 eggs
1 quart buttermilk
3/4 teaspoon baking soda
7-1/2 cups cake flour
1/2 pound bitter chocolate, melted
1/2 teaspoon vanilla

Cream margarine and sugar, add eggs, mix buttermilk and soda together. Then add alternately with flour to mix. Pour in melted chocolate and vanilla and mix thoroughly. This recipe will make two cakes. Bake at 350 degrees until thoroughly cooked, about twenty to twenty-five minutes. Ice with chocolate icing. To make Wellesley Fudge Cake, add chopped pecans to batter and sprinkle on top of cake after icing.

NOTES

SETTING UP SHOP

1. Telephone interview with Richard Hutzler, July 3, 2009.
2. *Abram G. Hutzler: His Book* (Baltimore: Hutzler Bros., 1921).
3. *The Mercantile Career of the Hutzler Family* (Baltimore: Johns Hopkins University, 1939).
4. Ibid.

BUILDING A PALACE

5. *Abram G. Hutzler.*
6. *Mercantile Career of the Hutzler Family.*
7. *Tips and Taps*, March 1921.
8. Francis F. Bierne, *Hutzler's: A Picture History* (Baltimore: Hutzler Bros., 1968).
9. *Tips and Taps*, "Hutzler's Timeline," 1963.

THE GLORY DAYS

10. *Baltimore Sun*, October 11, 1931.
11. *Mercantile Career of the Hutzler Family.*
12. *Tips and Taps*, July 1942.
13. Bierne, *Hutzler's*, 15.
14. *Tips and Taps*, "Hutzler's Timeline," 1968.

SHOPPING AROUND

15. Jewish Museum of Maryland, *Enterprising Emporiums: The Jewish Department Stores of Downtown Baltimore* (Baltimore: Jewish Museum of Maryland, 2001), 9–11.
16. "Maryland 50th Anniversaries, 1897–1947," Calendar (Baltimore: Hochschild, Kohn & Co., 1947).
17. Ibid.
18. Ted Shelsby, "Hochschild Will Close Downtown Store in July; Sales Are Off, Subway Coming," *Baltimore Sun*, January 22, 1977.
19. Jewish Museum of Maryland, *Enterprising Emporiums*, 25–26.
20. Peter B. Peterson, *The Great Baltimore Fire* (Baltimore: Maryland Historical Society, 2004).
21. Adele M. Hicks, "O'Neill's and Its Gentlemanly Owner," *Baltimore Sun Magazine*, December 2, 1979.
22. Peterson, *Great Baltimore Fire*.
23. Jewish Museum of Maryland, *Enterprising Emporiums*, 30–31.
24. Hecht Company Annual Report, 1945.
25. Bob Liston, "Hecht, May Firms Merger Boost to Downtown," *Baltimore American*, February 1, 1959.

THE RIGHT STORE, THE RIGHT PLACE, THE RIGHT TIME

26. George Hutzler Bernstein, telephone interview by author, June 23, 2009.
27. "Ground Broken for Hutzler's Towson," *Baltimore Sun*, June 23, 1950.
28. "Suburban Age Reflected in Department Store," *Evening Sun*, November 21, 1952.
29. Jacques Kelly, "Towson Hutzler's Dining Offers Tasty Isle of Tradition in Suburban Triangle," *Evening Sun*, March 24, 1987.

THE SALE OF THE CENTURY

30. *Tips and Taps*, January 1943.
31. Interview with Jacques Kelly, June 27, 2009.
32. Ibid.
33. Rob Kasper, "Shopping Tradition Lives On," *Baltimore Sun*, November 28, 1980.
34. *Tips and Taps*, "Hutzler's Timeline," 1968.
35. Interview with Dan and Sue Sachs, June 23, 2009.

We Are Not a Tree

36. Ibid.
37. "New Store to Be Opened by Hutzler's—Company Also Plans to Enlarge Facility at Eastpoint," *Baltimore Sun*, August 30, 1964.
38. Interview with Jacques Kelly, June 27, 2009.
39. Interview with Lynn Stecher Cox, July 3, 2009.
40. *Baltimore News American*, October 10, 1965.
41. Interview with Dan and Sue Sachs, July 1, 2009.

Occasion Extraordinaire

42. Interview with Dan and Sue Sachs, June 23, 2009.
43. *Tips and Taps*, "Hutzler's Timeline," 1968.
44. Ibid.
45. Interview with Dan and Sue Sachs, June 23, 2009.
46. Ibid.

A Gift from Hutzler's Means More

47. "Hutzler's Towson Store Opens Nov. 24th," *Baltimore Magazine*, November 1952.
48. Telephone interview with Dan Sachs, July 24, 2009.
49. Telephone interview with Sue Sachs.

The Best of Everything

50. Telephone interview with Gilbert Sandler, July 28, 2009.
51. Ibid.

Society Page

52. Interview with Bob Eney, July 1, 2009.
53. Interview with Dan and Sue Sachs, July 1, 2009.
54. "Secrets of a Seaport," Preservation Society of Fell's Point and Federal Hill, 2007.

55. Jewish Museum of Maryland, *Enterprising Emporiums*, 50–51.
56. Ibid.
57. Interview with Sue Sachs, June 23, 2009.
58. Telephone interview with Albert D. Hutzler III, June 28, 2009.
59. Ibid.

Family Business

60. *Tips and Taps*, July 1971.
61. Telephone interview with George Hutzler Bernstein, June 24, 2009.
62. *Tips and Taps*, December 1972.
63. Interview with Dan and Sue Sachs, June 23, 2009.
64. Interview with Sue Sachs, July 1, 2009.
65. *Tips and Taps*, April 1974.
66. "Union Reports of Layoff of Substantial Number of Hutzler Employees," *Evening Sun*, July 31, 1976.
67. Telephone interview with David A. Hutzler, June 30, 2009.
68. "The Demise of Stewart's Downtown, Why?" *Baltimore News American*, January 3, 1979.
69. "Downtown Stewart's Will Close," *Baltimore Sun*, January 3, 1979.
70. Gilbert Sandler, *Small Town Baltimore* (Baltimore: Johns Hopkins University Press, 2002).
71. Ted Shelsby, "Hochschild Will Close Downtown Store in July; Sales Are Off, Subway Coming," *Baltimore Sun*, January 22, 1977.
72. William H. Jones, "Hochschild to Close Baltimore Store," *Washington Post*, January 22, 1977.
73. Interview with Dan and Sue Sachs, June 23, 2009.

Under New Management

74. Interview with Dan and Sue Sachs, July 1, 2009.
75. Interview with Bob Eney, July 1, 2009.
76. "Hutzler's 'Palace' Building to Be Condemned in Renewal," *Baltimore News American*, September 29, 1977.
77. Michael K. Hirten, "Hutzler's Hoping Harbor Store Will Add Luster to Downtown," *Evening Sun*, February 29, 1980.
78. Interview with Dan and Sue Sachs, July 1, 2009.

79. Stacie Knable, "Hutzler's Wants to Have that Royal Feeling Again," *Evening Sun*, August 6, 1981.
80. Interview with Dan and Sue Sachs, July 1, 2009.
81. Knable, "Hutzler's Wants…"

MAKING CHANGE

82. Stacie Knable, "Downtown Hecht Goes Suburban," *Evening Sun*, September 22, 1982.
83. *Baltimore Sun*, Editorial, "Stewart's," November 9, 1982.
84. Jessie Glasgow, "Hutzler's Gets New President, New Capital," *Baltimore Sun*, May 17, 1983.
85. David Brown, "Downtown Hutzler's to Move to New Atrium Complex," *Baltimore Sun*, August 19, 1983.
86. Scott Duncan, "Hutzler's Trying to Be the Best," *Evening Sun*, August 22, 1984.
87. Ellen Uzelac, "Hutzler's Hustles to Gain on Hecht," *Baltimore Sun*, November 25, 1984.

EVERYTHING MUST GO

88. Derek Reveron, "Shoppers Eye Glitter, Prices," *Evening Sun*, April 2, 1985.
89. Telephone interview with David A. Hutzler, June 30, 2009.
90. "Westminster to Get Smaller Hutzler's," *Baltimore News American*, August 13, 1985.
91. Telephone interview with David A. Hutzler, June 30, 2009.
92. Telephone interview with Richard Hutzler, July 3, 2009.
93. Ted Shelsby, "Hutzler's to Close Downtown Store If Rent Isn't Reduced," *Baltimore Sun*, June 9, 1987.
94. Joan Tyner, "Hutzler's Adds Pizzazz to Lure Back Customers—Local Retailer Faces Struggle to Survive," *Baltimore Sun*, November 11, 1987.
95. "Hutzler's Tea Room," *Towson Times*, October 12, 1988.
96. Jacques Kelly, "City's Shoppers Losing a Mecca," *Evening Sun*, September 15, 1988.
97. Sherrie Clinton, "Hutzler's Palace Is Going Discount," *Evening Sun*, September 21, 1988.
98. Sherrie Clinton, "Hecht's Downtown Store to Close to Stop Red Ink," *Evening Sun*, October 19, 1988.

99. Joan Tyner, "Downtown Hutzler's Closing Doors to Shoppers, Ending Era, at 6 pm," *Baltimore Sun*, February 18, 1989.

100. Sandler, *Jewish Baltimore*.

101. Ibid.

102. Telephone interview with Nancy Thorn, July 28, 2009.

103. Joan Tyner, "The Death of an Institution," *Baltimore Sun*, October 22, 1989.

104. Telephone interview with Nancy Thorn, July 28, 2009.

Closeout

105. Martin B. Kohn, *Hochschild, Kohn and Company—A Personal Account* (Baltimore: Hochschild Kohn & Co., 1979).

106. Paul Milton, "Mourning Hutzler's," *Towson Times*, October 18, 1989.

107. Telephone interview with Dan Sachs, June 16, 2009.

108. Interview with Dan and Sue Sachs, July 1, 2009.

109. Edward Gunes, "Disrespect for Deco in State's Hutzler Conversion," *Baltimore Sun*, March 2, 1986.

110. Interview with security, July 16, 2009.

ABOUT THE AUTHOR

Michael J. Lisicky is an oboist with the Baltimore Symphony Orchestra. Originally from southern New Jersey, he is a graduate of the New England Conservatory of Music in Boston. A certified tour guide for the Preservation Society of Fell's Point and Federal Hill, he currently serves as the towne crier of Fell's Point. Mr. Lisicky also helps run an "Ask the Expert" column on the website www.departmentstorehistory.net.

Visit us at
www.historypress.net